CONTENTS

WORKSIGHT No.16 2020

Photo：橋本裕貴

The Continued Future of

Smart Workplaces

CBA / Paramount House / Aurecon

Woodside / Arup / RMIT University

Quay Quarter Tower / Mirvac

続・スマートワークプレイスの未来

ABWとテクノロジーを融合させ、スマートワークプレイスを独自に発展させた
オーストラリア。前号の欧州とはまた異なる未来を目指すオーストラリアの
実践を8つの事例から紐解いていく。

※今号の記事は2019年に実施した取材に基づいて制作しました

巨大な谷を思わせるダイナミックな吹き抜け。三方を取り囲むオフィスに、トップライトから自然光が差し込む。視認性を高めることで職場全体のエネルギーを感じられるしかけ。

CASE 1

「人」の力でデジタル分野ナンバーワンを目指す
豪州最大のメガバンク

CBA
［シービーエー］

Australia's largest mega-bank aims to be number one
in digital through people power

カフェテリア。食事をとる者もいれば、PCで作業をする者も。カフェテリアに限らず、内装は木材を多用した温かみのあるトーン。植栽の数も3,800点を超える。

エントランス近くの、ワーカー向け作業スペース兼リラックス・スペース。オープンスペースの多かったABWを洗練させ、コラボレーションをサポートするために設けられた。

オフィス外観。フロアあたりの面積は約6,000㎡だ。「サッカー場より少し広いといえばわかりやすいでしょうか」（リー氏）

上階から見下ろしたGF（地上階）の「プラザ」には、カフェやミーティングルームなど、人が交流するスポットを集めた。ゲストも社員とともに使うことができる。

吹き抜け越しに、各フロアで働くワーカーの様子を見渡せる。自分がどこにいても人の動きや存在を視覚的に感じられる構造。

CBA

シドニー
創業：1911年
従業員数：4万8,238人（2019年）
総資産：9,765億オーストラリアドル（2019年）

1／オフィスの入退室やロッカーは
自社開発のアプリで管理。ファシ
リティの不具合が見つかれば壁に
あるQRコードからその場で報告す
ることができる。これにより効率
的なファシリティマネジメントが可
能になる。

2／どこで誰が仕事をしているのか、
PCをLANケーブルにつなぐこと
で位置を把握することができる。
集められたデータは利用頻度など
を参考にファシリティの数や位置
を改善するのに活用される。

約5万人の従業員を擁するオーストラリア・コモンウェルス銀行（Commonwealth Bank of Australia／CBA）は、豪州最大の銀行だ。その新オフィス「CBA Axle」はシドニー市内に点在していた拠点を再開発エリア「サウス・イヴリー」に集約することを意図したもの。「デジタル分野でナンバーワンの銀行になる」との経営戦略を掲げる同行は、社員同士の距離を近づけコラボレーションを促そうと考えた。延床面積4万3,000㎡、フロア当たり6,000㎡のオフィスに約4,000名が勤務する。はす向かいに新たにオープンするビルも合わせれば1万人をこのエリアに集める予定だ。

もっとも、これだけの広さになると単一のオフィスというよりシティキャンパスと捉えるのがふさわしい。「素晴らしいデザインの建物だけでなく、素晴らしい場所そのものをつくることが目標でした」と話すのは、ワークプレイスのデザインを担当した設計事務所ウッズバゴットのシニア・アソシエイト、ブラッドリー・リー氏だ。サウス・イヴリーには、スケートパークにテニスコート、バスケットコートにツリーハウスと、地域に開かれたスペースがふんだんに設けられている。CBAが運営するキッチンスペースで得られた収益も、すべてチャリティに寄付されているという。

「つまり、私たちは地域における『良き隣人』でありたいと思っているんです」と語るのは、CBAのエグゼクティブ・マネージャーを務めるローレンス・チェン氏だ。このようにプレイスメイキングに積極的な企業は、若者たちの目にも魅力的に映る。近隣にあるシドニー大学やニューサウスウェールズ大学から難なく人材を集められるのはそのためだろう。彼ら若き才能こそ、デジタル分野ナンバーワンを目指すCBAにとって最良のアセットとなるのは言うまでもない。

「勤務後にジムや病院、ショッピングセンターに行きたいと思えばすべてが近くにある。これらすべてが、よい職場づくりにおいての重要な要素となっています」（チェン氏）。ワークプレイスは単なる仕事場ではない、ということなのだろう。

建物内に目を転じよう。GF（地上階）のプラザは社外のワーカーも含めて自然と人が集まり、コラボレーションが誘発される場所だ。上階のオフィスにはABWが導入された。ABWにも人の自由な移動とコラボレーションを促す狙いがあるが、オープンプランにすれば十分とはしなかった。例えばワーカーの性格の問題。内向的で協業を得意としないワーカーからもコラボレーションを引き出すにはどうすればいいか。周囲がにぎやかでも、匿名的に、静かに仕事ができる場所が必要だ。カーテンやブースで仕切り、プライバシー重視のスペースを確保したのはそのためだ。

実は、彼らが実践するABWはこれが2.5世代目だという。第1世代は7〜8年前に始めた単純なオープンオフィス、第2世代は目的に合ったオープン主体の多様なワークプレイスを準備。しかしそれだけではワーカーのパフォーマンスを引き出せないとして、新たに第2.5世代では内向的／外向的という人々の性格まで加味したというわけだ。

「ABWは柔軟性を生み、スタッフのエンパワーメントとエンゲージメントを高めました。働き方

や場所に対する選択肢は、ワーカーへのアンケートの中でも毎回、CBAで働く最も大きなメリットとして挙げられています」（チェン氏）

最新のテクノロジーがそれと目立つことはないが、昨今のスマートワークプレイスらしく、入館の受付や席の予約などは自前のアプリを通じて行う。デジタルバンクを目指す彼らはワーカーにも最高のデジタルUXを提供しており、そのデータは建物内の利用効率や施設の利用頻度の把握に使われるという。

「データを見ることができるので、各階で使われていないスポットを把握できます。例えば、あるデスクが6カ月間ほとんど使われていないというデータがあったとします。ヒートマップのデータを通してそのデスクが壊れていたとか、何らかの理由が見つかるわけです」（チェン氏）

ここは人が自由に柔軟に働くためのキャンパス。それも、ベビーブーマーからジェネレーションX、ミレニアル世代まで全世代、またさまざまな障がいを抱えたワーカーも働く場所だ。その意味で彼らはテックジャイアントとは違うインクルーシブネスを求められる。「ミレニアル世代にアピールするためだけの単なるクールなデザイン」（リー氏）はあり得ない。

スタッフが変化に適応できるよう、デザイン作業は慎重に行われた。中には自分のオフィスやワークステーションに慣れ親しんできたスタッフもいる。彼らは自分専用のデスクを失ったのだ。しかし、ワークスペースの計画の展開について定期的にスタッフに知らせることで、「取り残された」と感じるワーカーがいないことが確認できた。このキャンパスは地域のもの。そしてすべてのワーカーのものなのだ。**WS**

新しいイノベーション・ディストリクト「サウス・イヴリー」

シドニー郊外にある「サウス・イヴリー」は、かつて蒸気機関車の工場で栄えたエリア。オーストラリアを前進させた多くのインフラはここでつくられた。時を経て一度は廃れたこの街だが、いまは不動産デベロッパーであるマーバック（Mirvac／72ページ参照）、そしてAMPキャピタルとサンスーパー、センチュリア・プロパティ・ファンドとのコンソーシアムの手による再開発の途上にあり、オーストラリアの新しいイノベーション・ディストリクトとして、再び多くの人を引きつけようとしている。テニスコートや農場など、各種スポーツ施設やレクリエーション施設を多くの人々が楽しむエリアとしても注目される。いずれスーパーマーケットや美容院、ジム、屋外カフェなどが混在する9つの商業ビルが完成する予定だ。シドニーの先住民「ガディガル」に敬意を払い、地域コミュニティとのつながりを重視しているのも特徴の1つである。

© Eberle Photography

1／ファシリティチームが主に使う
エリア。ベーシックなデスクのほか、
昇降式のデスクが確認できる。巨
大なホワイトボードには、フロアの
ディバイダー（仕切り）の役割も。
家具類は既製品ではなくカスタム
メイド中心。

2／オフィス中央にある階段状に
座席が並んだシアタースペース。
毎日のようにイベントが催され、に
ぎわいをオフィス全体に届けている。
取材当日は「健康的な食事」をテー
マにしたセミナーが行われていた。

3／デザインも動線も流線的。「自
然界に『直線』はありませんから」（リ
ー氏）。この天井も流線的なデザイ
ンを取り入れている。多くの植栽
とともに自然からヒントを得たバイ
オフィリック・デザインが随所に施
されている。

シービーエー
コマーシャル・デザイン＆
デリバリー・グループ
エグゼクティブ・マネージャー
ローレンス・チェン

Lawrence Chan
Executive Manager
Commercial Design &
Delivery Group
CBA

ウッズバゴット
シニア・アソシエイト
ブラッドリー・リー

Bradhly Le
Senior Associate
Woods Bagot

1

3

2

4

1／ABWでの働き方に慣れ、適応できるよう、入社したばかりの新しいワーカーには特別なトレーニングが施される。

2／エントランス近くのラウンジスペース。社員や社外の人とのコラボレーションを誘発する目的でGF（地上階）近くにコミュニケーションスペースを集中させている。

3／「パーゴラ」と呼ばれる執務エリアに置かれたコミュニケーション・ハブ。ドリンクやスナックなどでワーカー同士をつなげる役割を果たす。

4／スケートパークをはじめとするパブリックスペースを周囲に用意した。地域、オフィスとは遊歩道で結ばれ、ビジネスとコミュニティのつながりが示されている。

サウス・イヴリー内、CBA Axleのはす向かいに2021年完成予定の新しいビル（延床面積約5万5,000㎡）。「オーストラリアで1番か2番の広さの建物になる予定です」（チェン氏）。完成次第、CBAのデジタル系スタッフが移動し、CBA Axleと合計で1万人が勤務する予定だ。

GF（地上階）のプラザ。手前にあるのはカフェスタンドだが、奥のラウンジやシアタースペースとの間に境界らしい境界が見当たらない。ノンテリトリアルな人の移動を促す狙い。

CASE 2

「ポストコード2010」の住人が集う
クリエイティブ・コミュニティ

Paramount House
[パラマウント・ハウス]

A gathering place for the creative community
of postcode 2010

カフェ「パラマウント・コーヒー・プロジェクト」。独自のカフェ文化を発達させたオーストラリアでは、朝からビジネスパーソンがコーヒーカップを片手にミーティングする姿が珍しくない。

FIRE INDICATOR
PANEL

パラマウント・ハウスの中で最初に誘致したテナントがパラマウント・コーヒー・プロジェクト。のちに、映画館、バー、最上階にある広告会社のワークスペースと続いた。地域コミュニティの中心だ。

カフェのエントランス付近。訪れるのは「徒歩5分で来られる」地元の住民ばかり。パラマウント・ハウスのワーカーもほとんどがこのエリアに居住しているという。朝はビジネスミーティングが多い。

「どのテナントを選ぶにも、ベストな質を求めました」（バートン氏）との自負がここにはある。リラックスのため、仕事のため、各人が思い思いの時間を過ごせるカフェだ。

パラマウント・ハウス最上階に入居している広告会社のワークスペース。このコミュニティの雰囲気に惹かれ入居を決めたという。

パラマウント・ハウスの外観。右奥に見えるのが、かつてパラマウント・ピクチャーズのオーストラリア本社として使われていたアールデコ調の建物だ。

屋上階にはカフェやヨガスタジオ、マッサージルームを併設する「パラマウント・レクリエーション・クラブ」がある。フィットネスクラブはメンバーシップ制だが、カフェは出入り自由。

Paramount House
シドニー
開業：2014年

ホテルの客室の中には、小さなイ
ンナーバルコニーを備えた部屋も
ある。ルーバーからは乾いた風と
自然光が差し込む。

1／パラマウント・ハウスに入居する「パラマウント・ハウス・ホテル」。客室は29部屋、1つとして同じデザインの部屋がない。「Sunny」と名付けられたこの部屋はフレンチリネンのシーツ、テラゾーのバスルーム、植物で満たされたアルコーブが売り。

2／パラマウント・ハウス・ホテルのレセプション。オーストラリア出身の芸術家の作品が飾られている。カウンターに備えられたタップからウェルカムドリンクとして炭酸水、コンブチャ、ビールを選べる。

3／パラマウント・ハウスのサイン。控えめで洗練されたグラフィックやサインがそこかしこに施されている。目立つのではなく、地域に溶け込もうという意志を感じ取れる。

カフェやセレクトショップが立ち並ぶ情報感度の高い街、サリーヒルズ。ここに、1970年代初頭までオーストラリアの映画文化の象徴とされた建物が立ち並んでいる。かつての持ち主はパラマウント・ピクチャーズと20世紀フォックス。インターネット前史のこと、通りを行き交う人々は、レンガ造りの美しい建物を見上げるたび華やかなハリウッドを想像した。だが2つの会社が退去してから30年余り、テナントの業績がふるわない時代が続いた。

そんな不遇の建物を地域のクリエイティブ・コミュニティを育む複合施設「パラマウント・ハウス」として蘇らせたのは、新たに建物を購入したデベロッパーと、デザインを担当した都市開発コンサルティング・エージェンシーのライト・アングル・スタジオだ。彼らは過去のテナントが根付かなかった反省を踏まえ、カフェ、映画館、バー、スポーツクラブ、コワーキングと、慎重に1つずつ選んだ。

「こうした手法はオーストラリアでは珍しい」とライト・アングル・スタジオのディレクター、バリー・バートン氏は言う。「通常はもっとタイトなスケジュールで、ほとんどの建物は一度にテナントを選びます」（バートン氏）

最初に決まったテナントはカフェ「パラマウント・コーヒー・プロジェクト」だ。「サリーヒルズの人々は毎日コーヒーを飲みますから」と、上質なコーヒーを提供すれば新しいコミュニティが生まれ連鎖的に成功すると確信していた。協力的な姿勢かどうかもテナント選びのポイント。建物内では多くの人々がそれぞれにコミュニティを構成する。スペースを共有する意識を持ち、友好的な関係を築けるテナントを探した。テナントがすべて決まるまで8年の歳月が費やされたが、こうして街に根付いたことを思えば苦労の甲斐はあった。

そもそも公共交通機関が発達していないシドニーは、旅行者にはあまり向かない街だとバート

ン氏は考えている。「東京のように山手線がありませんからね」。ここを訪れるのも、多くが近隣住民。それも建物と同じ「ポストコード（郵便番号）2010」のエリアで暮らす「ネイバーズ（隣近所）」だ。サリーヒルズはオーストラリアでも指折りの人口密集地。小さなアパートで暮らす若い単身世帯が多く、徒歩5分で行けるシドニーの中心部で働いている。いつも新しいことやおもしろいことを探している彼らのことだ。パラマント・ハウスに目をつけるのは当然のなりゆきだったことだろう。またパラマウント・ハウスのように、コミュニティを重視し、地域に対して責任を持つ企業はミレニアル世代の価値観とも重なる。

「55歳より上の世代の方々は若年世代とは考え方が異なると捉えています。若者には常にインターネットがあり、フェイスブックやインスタグラムなどのコミュニティの中で他人との関係性を意識しています。彼らは気候変動や同性婚など、さ

まざまな価値観を発信し、人々と共有したいと考えているのです」（バートン氏）

　ワークスペース1つとっても、ミレニアル世代の価値観は反映されている。彼らはただ働く環境さえあればいいとは考えない。コワーキングスペースを手がけたジ・オフィス・スペースのファウンダー、ナオミ・トシック氏は「『仕事へ行く』ことが『教会に行く』ことの代わりになっている」と表現。「人々はスピリチュアルなものやコミュニティを求めてこの建物を訪れます。私たちはそのニーズに対して対応できているのではないでしょうか」。Netflixよりも映画館、Uber Eatsよりもカフェを好む彼らは、人と会いたがっている。それを妨げることがないよう、建物内にはニュートラルで洗練されたものしか置いていない。

　今、ライト・アングル・スタジオには、大企業からのオフィス設計の依頼がひっきりなしに舞い込んでいるという。彼らは一様に保守的で、それだけに若者を集められる新しい職場環境のアイデアを外部に求めている。

　「私たちのクライアントは、つねにさまざまなタイプのコンサルタントからアドバイスを受けています。その中でも私たちの意見は特殊なものでしょう。私たちはこの建物内の人々を観察し、クライアントへ伝えています。人々が何を求めているか、ほかのコンサルタントとは違った見解を述べられるのです。大企業のクライアントにとって、私たちはとても小さなアドバイザーかもしれません。でも、そんな会社だからこそ堂々と違う視点で意見を言えるのだと思います」（バートン氏）**WS**

1

2

3

4

1／テナントの1つ、ワインバー「Poly」。オーストラリアのワインを中心に気軽な価格帯で食事とドリンクを楽しめる。

2／コワーキングスペース「ジ・オフィス・スペース」。現在22社が入居する。各社が専用の個室を持ち、プライバシーを守りながら、共有スペースでの交流もある。アートにも力を入れている。

3／1930年代当時の試写室の趣を再現した映画館。週6回、夜に2本の映画が上映されている。日中は、ビジネス・プレゼンテーションやワークショップにも利用される。

4／映画館に併設されているバー。「ゴールデンエイジ・シネマ＆バー」と名付けられている。ライト・アングル・スタジオが運営。

5／コワーキングスペース内の個室。ティータイムになるとキッチンに姿を見せるワーカーも。居心地がよいのか、オープンから3年経っても顔ぶれは最初に入居した企業のまま。

6／「パラマウント・レクリエーション・クラブ」。24時間営業のフィットネスクラブだ。ヨガやボクササイズなど、週に220ものクラスを提供している。

5

6

ライト・アングル・スタジオ
ディレクター
バリー・バートン

Barrie Barton
Director
Right Angle Studio

ジ・オフィス・スペース
ファウンダー
ナオミ・トシック

Naomi Tosic
Founder
The Office Space

MAP / SCENES

オーストラリアは日本の約21倍という広大な国土を有し、気候風土は温帯、砂漠、熱帯と変化に富む。世界第2位の都市部に人口が集中（約90%）する国であり、都市のありようが国の文化・経済を育んでいる。ここでは取材で訪れた主要4都市のキャラクターに迫る。

Brisbane

Perth

Sydney

Melbourne

Melbourne

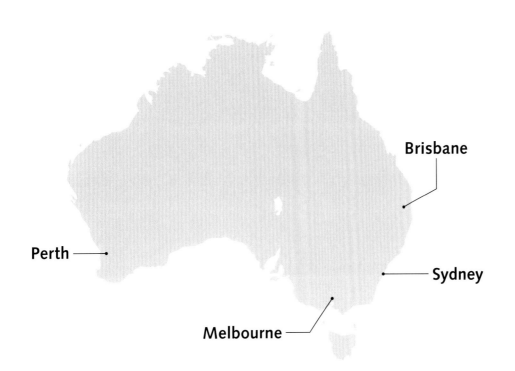

1 「Kings Domain」はヤラ川の南に広がる公園。小高い丘にある戦没者慰霊碑からはCBD（中央業務地区）のスカイスクレイパーが見える。

2 アートやストリートファニチャーなど豊かな公共空間がヤラ川沿いに広がる。この「Red Stair」はメルボルン市からのコミッションでつくられた。

3 オフィス周辺の屋外空間はランチタイムには多くのワーカーでにぎわう。

4 「Sandridge Bridge」は、ヤラ川に架かる歴史的な鉄道橋であり、2006年にパブリックアートをフィーチャーした新しい歩道としてリニューアルされた。

5 中心部のオフィスビルの足元には屋外空間が充実している。ランドスケープ・アーキテクトが社会的に尊敬されるオーストラリアならでは。

6 特有の魅力を持つメルボルンの路地（Laneway）にはグラフィティやインスタレーションなど多様なストリートアートが。

7 メルボルンで最も高いビルである「Eureka Tower」の展望台からCBDを望む。手前が古いCBD、左奥に再開発エリアのドックランズが広がる。

8 メルボルンを代表するカフェストリート「Centre Place」。通りに所狭しと客席が並ぶ、ワーカーの憩いの場だ。

9 メルボルンの中央駅「Southern Cross Station」から、ドックランズを望む。駅前物件が通勤の苦痛を軽減しウェルビーイングを高めると人気だ。

　オーストラリアの南東に位置するビクトリア州の州都メルボルンは、オーストラリア第2位の約500万人の人口を有する都市である。山と海に囲まれたシドニーとは違って拡張可能な平坦地が続くメルボルンは2025年にはシドニーを追い抜き国内第1位の人口になると予測されている。英エコノミスト誌の「The Global Liveability Index」では、2011年から7年間トップを獲得する世界的なライフスタイル都市としても知られ、人を惹き付ける原動力になっている。特に背後にワイン産地を抱える一流のフードシーン、カフェカルチャーは強調すべき点だろう。ダイバーシティのある都市として、60万人以上のアジア言語、50万人以上の英語以外のヨーロッパ言語を話す人々が存在し、260以上の言葉が話されている。ロンドン、

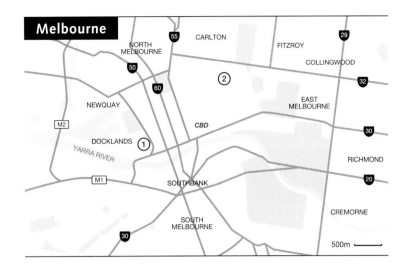

Melbourne

CARLTON 55
NORTH MELBOURNE 50 FITZROY 29
COLLINGWOOD
60 ② EAST MELBOURNE 32
NEWQUAY
CBD 30
M2 DOCKLANDS ①
YARRA RIVER RICHMOND
M1 20
SOUTHBANK
SOUTH MELBOURNE CREMORNE
30
500m

①

Arup
アラップ
メルボルン
創業：1946年
従業員数：約1万5,500人（2019年）
売上高：17億1,000万ポンド（2019年）
※各種データはグループ全体のもの

②

RMIT University
アールエムアイティー・
ユニバーシティ
メルボルン
設立：1887年
学生数：8万6,839人（2018年）

10 ヤラ川の橋の橋脚につくられた
カフェ「Ponyfish Island」。川を間
近に食事を楽しめるとあっていつ
も満席だ。

11 CBDの一部では自動車を排し、
トラム、歩行者、自転車などがシー
ムレスに展開されるゾーンが設け
られ、観光客や市民でにぎわう。

12 市民や観光客の足はトラム。中
心部では無料で運行され、経済活
性化に貢献。

13 豊かなカフェカルチャーが育ま
れる中で、最近の注目株は「Higher
Ground」。かつての発電所をコン
バートしてつくられたダイナミック
な空間が広がる。

ニューヨーク、パリに次ぐ多さで世界の学生が学
ぶ大学都市の側面もあり、メルボルン大学、モナ
シュ大学、RMITユニバーシティなどが国際的に
高い評価を確立している。近代的な大都市のイ
メージのシドニーと比べると歴史的な建物や文化
が残り、ヤラ川の北側に位置する19世紀末に骨
格がつくられた碁盤目状のCBDは、トラムなど公
共交通が無料で運行されており、世界有数のコ
ンパクトシティとしても知られる。CASEで紹介
するアラップは、再開発が進む新CBDであるド
ックランズに新居を構えた。RMITユニバーシテ
ィは古いCBDの北端に位置し、北にあるメルボ
ルン大学を結ぶエリアをメルボルン・イノベーシ
ョン・ディストリクトとする構想が動いている。
2026年には10カ年の都市成長戦略が完了する
見込みだ。市民の呼称は「メルバーニアン」。

ブリスベンは、クイーンズランド州の州都。シドニー、メルボルンに次ぐオーストラリア第3の都市であり、人口は約230万人。亜熱帯気候で、夏は暑くて湿度が高く、冬も寒くない。国内ではダーウィンに次ぐ2番目に暑い都市だ。CBDはブリスベン川の半島部に位置し約2.2km²である。ヴィクトリア女王に敬意を表したクイーン・ストリートは、ブリスベンの伝統的な中心街となっており、歩行者専用道路となっているクイーン・ストリート・モールがショッピング街としてにぎわう。中心部

の人口密度は1km²あたり400人に近く、シドニーのそれに匹敵する。

伝統的にブリスベンは、シドニーやメルボルンに本拠地を構える大企業の支社・支店が集中する、いわゆる「支店経済」のような性質を有している。オーレコンはCBDの北端1.6kmにある再開発エリア「ブリスベン・ショーグラウンド」に拠点を構える。この再開発では、1万5,000人が暮らし、仕事をし、遊ぶための場所がミックスされた職住近接型のエリアを目指している。

1 ストーリー橋のたもとにある「Howard Smith Wharves」。1930年代の不況時に地元住民に救援活動を行った建築はいまやリテールやレストランが並ぶヒップなスポットに。

2 スワン川南岸に走るペデストリアンではローラーブレード、シェアキックボードなど多様な移動風景が。

3 「Streets Beach」はサウスバンクの象徴であり、オーストラリアで唯一の都心にある人工ビーチ。

4 「Queen Street Mall」は中心部に延びる歩行者専用モール。約500mに及ぶモールには6つのショッピングセンターはじめ700以上のリテールが。

5 温暖な気候が豊かな亜熱帯植物を育てる。至るところで、木陰で休む市民やワーカーの姿が見られた。

Brisbane

③
Aurecon
オーレコン
ブリスベン
創業：2009年
従業員数：約7,500人（2019年）

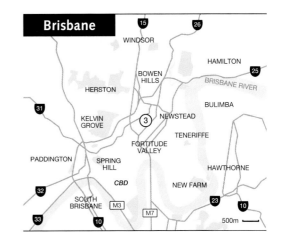

Brisbane
WINDSOR
HAMILTON
BOWEN HILLS
HERSTON
BRISBANE RIVER
BULIMBA
KELVIN GROVE
NEWSTEAD
TENERIFFE
PADDINGTON
FORTITUDE VALLEY
SPRING HILL
HAWTHORNE
NEW FARM
CBD
SOUTH BRISBANE
500m

オーストラリア南東部、ニューサウスウェールズ州の州都。国内最大の500万人以上の人口を有し、南半球を代表する世界都市及び金融センターである。世界有数のレストラン、リテール、ホテルがある国際的な観光都市でもあり、海に臨むオペラハウスなどはよく知られている。市民の主な交通手段は自動車で、シドニー都市圏を環状に形成するメトロード（地図上ではMと記載）は、重要な道路網である。2007年にプレイスメイキングの分野で知られる都市学者のヤン・ゲール氏をCBDのリニューアルのディレクターに採用し、新しいライトレールの計画、新しいフェリー、より多くの都市緑化やサイクルレーンが誕生した。

CBDはシドニー湾に面した北部に集中し、特に巨大再開発エリア「バランガルー」は、オフィス、リテール、レジデンス、ホテル、カジノ、公園など複合的かつ環境配慮されたエリアが展開されている。古い金融街とオペラハウスなど文化施設が並ぶサーキュラー・キーにはキー・クォーター・タワーが建設され、一帯の雰囲気を新たなものに変えようとしている。CBDから南には蒸気機関車の巨大工場を改修した再開発エリア「サウス・イヴリー」があり、CBAがテックキャンパスを建設中だ。ビルズなど世界的なレストランが並ぶヒップな住宅街サリーヒルズには、映画産業の遺構をコンバージョンしたパラマウント・ハウスがある。

Sydney

Sydney

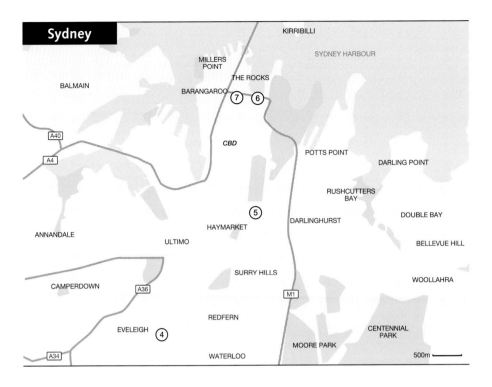

KIRRIBILLI
SYDNEY HARBOUR
MILLERS POINT
THE ROCKS
BARANGAROO
⑦ ⑥
CBD
BALMAN
POTTS POINT
DARLING POINT
RUSHCUTTERS BAY
DARLINGHURST
DOUBLE BAY
HAYMARKET
ULTIMO
BELLEVUE HILL
ANNANDALE
⑤
SURRY HILLS
WOOLLAHRA
CAMPERDOWN
REDFERN
CENTENNIAL PARK
EVELEIGH ④
MOORE PARK
WATERLOO
500m

④
CBA
シービーエー
シドニー
創業：1911年
従業員数：4万8,238人（2019年）
総資産：9,765億オーストラリアドル
（2019年）

⑤
Paramount House
パラマウント・ハウス
シドニー
開業：2014年

⑥
Quay Quarter Tower
キー・クォーター・タワー
シドニー
デベロッパー：AMPキャピタル
竣工：2022年
延床面積：10万2,000㎡

⑦
Mirvac
マーバック
シドニー
創業：1972年
従業員数：1,540人（2019年）

1 自然に囲まれたライフスタイルを好むシドニー市民は、オフィス前の芝生でも自由に寝転がる。

2 オーストラリア最大の巨大再開発エリアであるバランガルー。オフィス、リテール、レジデンス、ホテル、カジノ、公園など複合開発が進む。

3 バランガルーの玄関である地下鉄駅「Wynyard Station」。キャノピーは近未来のイメージを感じさせる。

4 オーストラリア出身の巨匠建築家ハリー・シードラー氏。彼が手がけたモダンビルディングのマスターピース「Australia Square Tower」。

5 バランガルーの超高層オフィスビル「International Towers」は建築家リチャード・ロジャース氏の設計。足元にはヒューマンスケールの空間が。

6 都市公共交通が脆弱なシドニー。クルマ社会を脱するため、トラム「Sydney Light Rail」を拡張。

7 オーストラリアに初めて入植者が辿りついたサーキュラー・キー。オペラハウスはじめ多くの文化施設、歴史を刻んだビジネス街が広がる。

8 ウィンヤード駅にある「Interloop」。古い木製エスカレーターを再構成した芸術家クリス・フォックス氏の作品。

Perth

⑧
Woodside
ウッドサイド
パース
創業：1954年
従業員数：3,823人（2019年）
売上高：3億4,300万ドル（2019年）

パースは西オーストラリア州の州都で、人口は約200万人でブリスベンに続く国内第4位、西オーストラリアを代表する大都市である。周辺に都市はなく、世界で最もほかの主要都市から離れた都市として知られる。

民族的なダイバーシティは高いが、ほかの国内主要都市の中でイギリス生まれの移民の割合が最も高い。地中海性気候であり、夏は暑く乾燥しており、冬の寒さは厳しくないが雨は比較的多い。

西部の郊外には最富裕層の住宅街があり、中心部から南北に離れた郊外は「住宅ローンベルト」と呼ばれる低・中級住宅街が広がる。スワン川沿いに中心地が形成され、聖ジョージ通り（セントジョージテラス）とアデレード通り（アデレードテラス）沿いに展開する碁盤目状のCBDの中央にウッドサイドが新本社屋を構えている。CBDにはキャットバスと呼ばれる無料バスが走っており、市民の足となっている。**WS**

Perth

MOUNT LAWLEY
60 53
65
NORTH BRIDGE
SUBIACO 8
⑧ CBD
61
66
EAST PERTH
KINGS PARK
SWAN RIVER
⑤ ②
500m

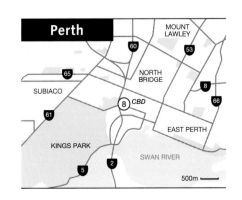

世界最大級の木造オフィスビルは
ワーカーのもう1つの「家」

Aurecon
［オーレコン］

One of the world's largest timber office buildings
is a second home to workers

1F（日本の2Fに該当）レセプション。オフィス内と変わらないオープンでリラックスできる空間。レセプションデスクではなくコンシェルジュを置いたのも、親しみやすさの演出だ。

2Fオフィスフロアも木材の雰囲気が強調されている。普通の高さのデスク、低いデスク、昇降式のデスクなど、ワーカーのニーズに応えるデスクが用意されている。

木材には、CLT（Cross Laminated Timber）を使用。部材はデベロッパーであるレンドリース自身が立ち上げた材料メーカーから供給されており、木材建築に対する本気度が伝わってくる。

　ブリスベンのCBD（中央業務地区）から1.6kmの距離に、デベロッパー大手レンドリースによる巨大再開発「ショーグラウンド」が進められている。計画が立ち上がったその頃、建設エンジニアリング会社のオーレコンは、CBDにあったオフィスビルのリースが切れ、社員700人のための新しい場所を探していた。レンドリースとは過去、複数のプロジェクトをともにした縁がある。レンドリースとともに木造高層ビルの設計と建設に協力できることはオーレコンにとって渡りに船であり、同ビルの建築管理エンジニアリング、サステナビリティ・コンサルティング、構造設計などはオーレコンが手がけた。

　オーレコンが新オフィスに望んだのは、年月を経ても安全で強固な建物であること、スタッフが気持ちよく働けること、そして革新的なデザイン。各国で木造高層ビルの建設が進む昨今だが、高さ52m、現時点で世界最大級の木造オフィスビル「25 King」はすべての条件を満たしていた。

　何より大切にしたかったのは、ある種「エンジニアリング会社らしくない」親しみやすさだ。「職場に来てほっとする、また職場に着いたときより仕事が終わって家に帰るときのほうがリフレッシュされているような、『ホーム』のような空間をつくり出すこと」とオーレコンのシニア・プロジェクト・エンジニア、フィリップ・サール氏は言う。確かに木造ビルは「オフィスビル＝コンクリート」という冷たいイメージを覆してくれるものだ。都市の喧騒を少し離れた再開発エリアも雰囲気にマッチしていた。GF（地上階）部分を見ても「ホーム」の

静かに作業に集中するためのブース。ミーティングは禁止。ただし予約はできず、使いたい場合は早いもの勝ちになるそう。

フロア中央に位置するコミュニケーションハブ。一息入れに来たワーカーがコーヒーを飲み、サンドイッチを食べる姿が。インフォーマルな打ち合わせにも使われる。

「エントランスの階段がとても好きで、毎日使っています」。明るい階段はウェイスク氏のお気に入りだ。

1

2

Aurecon
ブリスベン
創業：2009年
従業員数：約7,500人（2019年）

1／通称「禅ルーム」。PCなどの
電子機器は持ち込み禁止。テクノ
ロジーを離れてリフレッシュするた
めの空間だ。ストレスを和らげると
される塗り絵なども置かれている。

2／オーストラリア先住民は会議の
首長を決めず、屈託のない意見を
交換することを良しとする。これを
ヒントに机を多角形にし、会議中の
ヒエラルキーを廃した。

至るところに植物が多く設けられていることが、「ホーム」を思わせる落ち着きをオフィスにもたらしている。

オーレコンの設計哲学

Authenticity
信頼

Bravery
勇気

Connection
関係性

Wellness
健康

Creation
創造

Poetry
詩的感覚

Passion
情熱

オーレコンの新オフィスにおける7つのキーワード。マインドフルネスに関する多くの用語が使われている点が、現代的なオフィスを反映している。ウェルネスに関しては、ビルがWELL認証のCore and Shellで最高レベルのプラチナ認定を受けている。これは木造建築では世界で初めてのケースであり、クイーンズランド州においてもこの認定を受けた初めてのビルとして知られている。

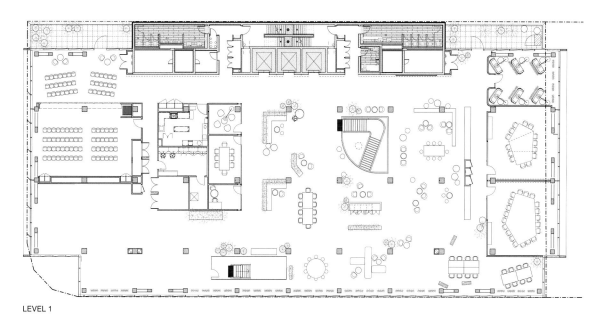

Scale 1 : 450

LEVEL 1

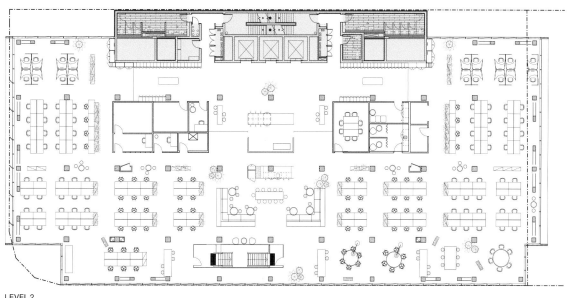

LEVEL 2

オフィスプランの一例。1F（日本の2Fに該当）はレセプションやミーティングルーム、2Fはワーカーのための標準的な執務スペースだ。

1

3

2

4

1／子ども用のアクティビティ・ルーム。オーストラリアには12歳以下の子どもを留守番させてはいけないという法律がある。子どもの学校が早く終わる日などはここで遊ばせる。取材時にはオフィス内にも子どもの姿が見られた。

2／1Fに常駐するコンシェルジュ。待ち構えるような受付ではなく、さりげなく来訪者をサポートする。ランプシェードはオーストラリア先住民のアーティストの作品。

3／ワーカーの健康にも配慮しようと、サービスカウンターには20種類以上のナッツやドライベリーなどが並べられていた。これらのヘルシーなスナックは血糖値を上げない間食としてオーストラリアでも注目されている。

4／ビルの共用部分、GF（地上階）のエレベーターホールの前には色鮮やかなグリーンが。ビルの共用設備として、大規模なバイクストレージも備える。

オーレコン
シニア・プロジェクト・エンジニア
ニコラス・ウェイスク

Nicholas Weiske
Senior Project Engineer
Aurecon

オーレコン
シニア・プロジェクト・エンジニア
フィリップ・サール

Phillip Saal
Senior Project Engineer
Aurecon

ウッズバゴット
アソシエイト・プリンシパル
サラ・マクマホン

Sarah McMahon
Associate Principal
Woods Bagot

建物外観。10階建て、建物の総面積は1万5,000㎡。使用された木材は、従来の建築材料よりもCO₂排出量が少なく、持続可能な形で管理された森林から調達したものだ。

意図は伝わってくる。家具がルーズに配置されたオープンスペース。家具を用途に合わせて自由に動かすことで、コミュニケーションをカジュアルに、スムーズにする。以前のオフィスと目立って違う点がもう1つある。オーレコンのオフィスの内装設計を担当した設計事務所ウッズバゴットのアソシエイト・プリンシパル、サラ・マクマホン氏によれば、最近のオーストラリアにはオフィスを高層階から低層階に移すことを望む傾向があるようだ。オーレコンの意向も同じだった。

「私たちはこのビルのアンカーテナント(建物の中核となるテナント)なので、開発業者のレンドリースは『オーレコンは最上階のオフィスを希望している』と考えていました。私たちは、『いや、(ストリートとの)交流を望んでいるよ』と」(オーレコンのシニア・プロジェクト・エンジニア、ニコラス・ウェイスク氏)

「ストリートから歩いて、そのままこの環境へと入ってくる、そのような体験を望んでいたのです」(サール氏)

事実、彼らはそのように働き始めた。転居以降、階段を使うワーカーが増えた。出社したスタッフはビル中央にある階段に向かい、窓からの朝日を浴びながら上階へ。ビルの真ん中に大きな階段を設けるのは大きなリスクを伴うプランだ。もし使われなかったらどれだけの投資が無駄になるのか。「でもフタを開けたら大成功でした。今で

はエレベーターに乗る人よりも階段を使う人のほうが圧倒的に多いです」(ウェイスク氏)

「ホーム」を感じさせるしかけは、ほかにもある。室内を照らすランプシェードはオーストラリア先住民のアーティストのもの。上座・下座のヒエラルキーを感じさせない多角形のテーブルも先住民の考え方にヒントを得たものだという。ABWもそうだ。マクマホン氏は「集中する必要がある場合はクワイエットスペースを探し、人と話し合う必要があればコラボレートできる場所を探す。ここのスペースは柔軟に対応できるところが素晴らしいと思います」と話す。オフィス空間の選択だけでなく、在宅やフレックスなど働き方に柔軟性があり、健康的な職場環境づくりを重要視しているのだ。エンジニアリング企業では驚異的だが、女性比率が40％近いという点もうなずける。

ある時、オフィスの内覧会が催され、300人ほどの見学者が集まったが、みな「エンジニアリング会社らしくない」と称賛した。もっとも、ここで働くワーカー以上にそれを強く実感している者はいないだろう。「カジュアルなスペースがおしゃべりにさせるのでしょうか」とサール氏。ウェイスク氏も続ける。「私は12年この会社で働いていますが、このビルに移った日、初対面の人の隣に座って『こんにちは、ニックです』とスムーズに自己紹介ができました。初日から誰もが、ここは人と会うのに適した環境だと感じたはずです」 **WS**

オフィスエントランス。ストリートに面したカフェは、外のライブ感あふれる雰囲気をオフィスに持ち込むためにつくられた。周辺の住宅、オフィスもグラウンドレベルのにぎわいをつくるよう工夫されている。

自然なテクノロジーでワーカーを支える
世界最高のスマートビル

Woodside

［ウッドサイド］

The world's greatest smart building
supports workers using naturalistic technology

ビルディングAにある19のフロア
をつなぐ階段。フロアごとに分断
されがちなワーカーの行き来を促し、
偶然の出会い〈bump〉をつくり出
す「バンプファクター」。単調にな
らないよう、複雑に構成されている

Woodside
パース
創業：1954年
従業員数：3,823人（2019年）
売上高：3億4,300万ドル（2019年）

世界最高レベルと呼ばれるスマートビルが
オーストラリア西部の観光都市パースに
ある。エネルギー大手ウッドサイドの本社ビルだ。
先住民の遺産に敬意を表し、かつての指導者の
名前から「Mia Yellagonga（ミア・ヤラゴンガ）」、
つまり「ヤラゴンガの場所」と名付けた。石油・ガ
スの埋蔵場所を探し当てるのがウッドサイドの事
業だ。テクノロジーの活用で競合に差をつけてい
たが、彼らは、ワークプレイスにもテクノロジーを
導入しようと考えた。それはスピーディに効率よ
く決断を下し、会社に未来をもたらすためである。
　「まず必要だったのは世界最高のベンチマーク
です」と語るのはワークプレイスの設計を手がけ
たユニスペースのグローバル・デザイン・ディレク
ター、サイモン・ポール氏。世界30カ所以上の最
新ビルを訪問し、アメニティ、サステナビリティ、
ウェルビーイング、ワークスペース、コネクティビ
ティ、そしてテクノロジーとイノベーションを1つ
のキャンパスに取り入れる方法を模索した。「彼
らは、このプロジェクトがこの先の15年を見据え
たものであることを望みました」。ビルのリースは
15年契約。ならばオフィスのコンセプトも15年の
間もちこたえるものにしなければならない。する
と「Mia Yellagonga」は15年先の未来のオフィス、
ということになる。
　特筆すべきは、ビル全体を統一的に管理する「テ
クノロジー・エコシステム」だ。これには同社の
ビジネスそのものが関わる。「Mia Yellagonga」
のプロジェクトが始まる3年前のこと。ウッドサ
イドは世界各地の精製プラントとそこを行き来す
る船や輸送列車からなるプラットフォームをスマ
ートに遠隔操業するために、AIを取り入れた。全
情報をIBMの「ワトソン」に放り込み、最適解を
導こうとしたのだ。続けて音声インターフェイス

「ファミリーゾーン」。ワーカーの家族ならいつでも利用可能。学校帰りの子どもが立ち寄り、宿題を済ませる。12歳以下の子どもだけで留守番させてはいけない法律があるこの国では重要な機能だ。健康的な食事を提供するレストランも完備。

1

2

4

3

5

1／エグゼクティブ用のフロア。以前は閉鎖的なオフィスで働いていた彼らだが、「情報をすばやく共有したい」との希望により個室を廃止し、オープンな仕様に刷新された。

2／「アドバンスド・オペレーション」。外部のパートナーが出入りできるスペース。AI、VRを活用してリアルタイムで3D設計を共有し、全員でスタディすることも可能だ。

3／クライアントをもてなすVIPルーム。フルコースを提供できるレストランも入っている。

4／テクノロジー・ハブ。ラップトップとスマートフォンで動き回るワーカーのために、ワンストップでIT機器の修理・交換などに応じてくれる。

5／低層階にある、ワーカーやその家族が利用できる「24／7 Cafe」。24時間365日アクセスでき、リラックスした作業環境を提供する。

「ラーニング・アンド・ウェルネス」フロア。研修用の部屋やライブラリー、仮眠スペースなどがある。「Wi-Fi not」スポットでもあり、テクノロジーから離れ心を休ませるデジタルデトックスの場所。

1

「ウィロー」を開発。アマゾンのアレクサなどのように、話しかければ答えてくれるコグニティブ・アシスタントだ。「石油やガスのこと、ビジネスのやり方などを学習させなければなりませんから」

このシステムを基盤に、シーメンスのミドルウェアなど各種のビルマネジメントシステムをつなぎ、統合したものが彼らの言うテクノロジー・エコシステム。ビルマネジメントにおいてもワトソンが最適な答えを導くのである。「Mia Yellagonga」が世界最高レベルのスマートビルたるゆえんだ。

例を挙げよう。テレビ／Web会議のシステムにはシスコの「スパーク」が導入されている。人数計測システムによりビル内のどこに何人いるのか察知可能だ。例えば12人用の会議室を5人で使用しているデータをワトソンに渡すとどうなるか。次回以降は別の会議室を使うよう指示を下し、大きな会議室は別のチームへ回すのだ。

もっとも「Mia Yellagonga」はテクノロジーをこれ見よがしにアピールするビルではない。むしろテクノロジーは自然で「見えないもの」であるよう配慮されている。入退館は非接触の生体認証（顔、指紋、静脈）を採用し、立ち止まることなくスムーズに通れる。センサーと専用アプリを通じてワーカー同士のリアルタイムの位置を把握することも可能だ。「テクノロジーはあくまで意思決定を手助けするものであり、目に入ってほしくないのです。ビルの中にはフレンドリーな雰囲気をつくりたい。そのためにウェルビーイングと仕事と生活のシナジーに力を入れました」とポール氏。

例えば、19フロアを階段でつなぎ、各階を行き来するワーカー同士の偶然の出会いを生み出す「バ

4つに分かれたフロア設計

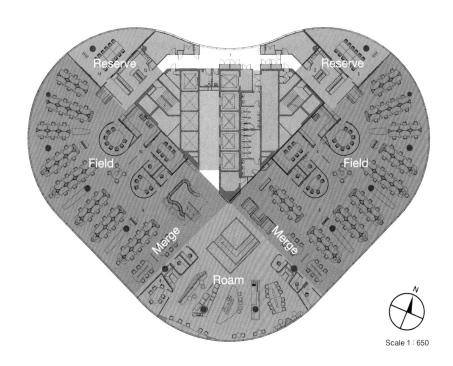

Scale 1 : 650

ビルディングAは10Fから27Fまでが標準仕様になっており、4つのスペースに分かれている。階段に接続されたフロア中央の「ローム」はインフォーマルなコラボレーションワークの場所。「リザーブ」はプロジェクトルーム。「マージ」は可変性のあるコラボレーションブース。「フィールド（写真）」は集中業務を行うための場所。

ンプファクター」。社員がオフィス内で自由に働く場所を選択できるよう、ワークスペースは可能な限りフレキシブルに。ユニスペースはワークスペースを4つのモードで捉えている。1人で作業に集中するフォーカスワーク・モード、他社とのコラボレーションワーク・モード、学習に重きを置いたラーニング・モード、同僚と交流するソーシャライジング・モード。それを1つのワークスペースでまかなえるものではない。彼らはABWやオープンスペースではなく「ライトスペース（正しい場所）」

というワークプレイス・フィロソフィーを掲げ、60以上の多様なワークセッティングを用意している。さらにインテリアには先住民の文化である6つの季節に応じたカラー、マテリアルの変化もつけている。ただでさえ、ウッドサイドで活躍するワーカーは多種多様。旧世代のエンジニアもいれば、大学を卒業したばかりの若いデータ・サイエンティストもいる。「だから異なる世代の人々が働くことができ、かつ将来を見据えたワークスペースをつくらなければならないのです」（ポール氏）**WS**

1／「Mia Yellagonga」はビルディングAからDまで4つの構造からなる。全32フロア、最大5,000人が働けるスペースに現在は約3,200人が働く。敷地内にはイノベーションセンター、リテールマーケット、アトリウム、チャイルドケアセンター、ウェルネスセンターなどが含まれる。

2／ビルディングB（写真）にはスポーツジムや研修施設など、ワーカーの学びや健康を支える施設がまとめられている。ビルディングCは大学など外部とのコラボレーションのための施設で、ビルディングDはNASA、MITとともに設計したロボティックスのラボを備えたビルだ。

2

ワーカーの満足度は飛躍的に向上

Rightspace	Utilization	Collaboration	Connectivity	Focus
アジャイルワークを採用した割合	デスクの利用率	部門の枠を超えたコラボレーションの頻度	技術の進化による「つながり」の向上	オフィスでの集中力の向上
0% → 92%	39% → 78%	40% → 65%	30% → 92%	60% → 60%

Pride	Wellbeing	Moral	Creative Thinking	Productivity
コミュニティ意識の向上	ウェルビーイングの向上	モチベーションの向上	イノベーションの向上	生産性や効率性の向上
62% → 92%	42% → 82%	64% → 82%	35% → 85%	200%up

「Mia Yellagonga」への入居から9カ月後にワーカーへ行ったPOE（入居前／入居後施設調査）の結果。コミュニケーション、コラボレーション、モチベーション、生産性※など多くの項目で数値が向上している。

※作業工程工学の測定結果をもとに、時間の半減を実現した

フレキシブルなワーカーが
自ら考えたビジョン「Living Arup」

Arup
［アラップ］

"Living Arup"
A user focused vision

Soundlab
Makerspace
Wellness Area
End of Trip Facility

3層のフロアと、それを緩やかにつ
なげる複数のメザニン（中間フロア）。
仕切りにガラスではなく金網を用
いることで視認性の向上とメンテ
ナンスフリーを実現している。

エントランスの横にあるワークラウンジ兼カフェスペース。社会的企業STREATに委託運営されており、恵まれない環境にいる若者をトレーニングし、社会復帰を促す場でもある。

オフィスの目前、地上11mにはスカイガーデン（空中庭園）が広がっており、昼時はワーカーたちの憩いの場になる。一帯の開発が完成すると規模がさらに拡大される予定だ。

Arup
メルボルン
創業：1946年
従業員数：約1万5,500人（2019年）
売上高：17億1,000万ポンド（2019年）
※各種データはグループ全体のもの

　ロンドン発のエンジニアリング、プランニング、デザイン会社アラップが、新しい働き方を提示している。3つのフロアを2つのメザニンでつなぐ構造もユニークだが、よりユニークなのは、独自のカルチャーだ。「（株式の）所有構造ですね。会社は従業員によって所有されているのです」とアラップのワークプレイス・リーダー、キャメロン・マッキントッシュ氏は言う。従業員が所有する組織として、アラップは外部の株主の意向に左右されず、実施するプロジェクトを自由に選択することができるのだ。また、エンジニアの会社としては珍しくABWを実践しているのも自らの発案だ。アラップは建築設計事務所ハッセルとともに2015年、オーストラリア地域のオフィス向けに、会社のフィロソフィーを踏まえた働き方

のガイドラインを開発した。それをどう導入するかは各拠点に委ねられている。ここメルボルンでは「Living Arup」というビジョンを掲げ、サステナビリティ、ウェルネス、コネクティビティ、フレキシビリティを重視すると決めた。

　彼らの新オフィスはその「Living Arup」の表現といえる。そして、それはまた彼らの横断的でフレキシブルなカルチャーをサポートする役割も果たすものだ。マネージャーはすべてのミーティングに参加し、プロジェクトでのすべての決定は彼らの議論を経て下された。「例えば500個のロッカーを『ロッカーの森』みたいに1つの場所に置くことについて、最初は緊張しましたが結果的にはうまくいきました」とマッキントッシュ氏は言う。

　3つのフロアを独立させるのではなく、複数の

建物外観。立地はオフィスビル、レジデンス、商業施設などからなるメルボルンの再開発エリア「メルボルン・クォーター」。その中のOne Melbourne Quarterに入居する。

1

2

3

アラップ
ワークプレイス・リーダー
キャメロン・マッキントッシュ

Cameron McIntosh
Workplace Leader
Arup

1／最上階のオフィススペース。ABWを運用しつつ部署ごとに大まかなゾーンが割り当てられている。4カ月に一度、ゾーンの入れ替えを行いコミュニケーションの固定化を防ぐ。

2／「ガーデン・ラウンジ」では自然光や風を感じながら打ち合わせが行える。600を超える植栽がオフィス内に置かれ、視覚的にも、新鮮な酸素供給の面でも健康を支える。大気汚染物質の屋内空気質も常にモニタリング。

3／スタッフがすぐに対応してくれる、ホスピタリティあふれるレセプション。奥に見えるのがカフェ兼ワークラウンジのSTREAT。

キッチンスペース。食事は各自の持ち寄りだが、フルーツやサラダはここで提供される。「今後は朝食の提供や料理教室なども検討しています」(マッキントッシュ氏)

4／500人分のロッカーを1カ所に集約。サポートセンターも併設されており、ワーカーはロッカーから私物を出し入れしにいくついでに、相談ごとを済ませてくる。

5／自転車通勤するワーカーが多いため、更衣室、シャワー、80台以上の自転車置き場などを備えたスペースを用意。オーストラリアではこうした設備は「エンド・オブ・トリップ・ファシリティ」と呼ばれている。

6／自社オフィス内の実験設備の充実も、新オフィスの大きな目的の1つだ。ここはさまざまな照明器具の状態をテストするライトラボ。

7／物件の建設前に空間の音響をテストするためのサウンドラボ。デザイン計画をまとめる前に効果を体験することができる。

8／レーザーカッターや3Dプリンターなどを置いたファブラボ。ワーカーが活用するが、高校生がエンジニアリングを学ぶ教育プログラムなどにも使われている。

4

5

6

7

8

メザニンを挟んだのは「3次元の体積」としてオフィスを捉えるため。2,000㎡の広さがあっても各フロアが視覚的につながっている。「個人的には2FからGF（地上階）までコーヒーを取りにいくのは面倒ですが、ビジネスや健康から考えたらいいことだと思います」（同氏）。執務エリアはゾーン別のグループアドレスとしているが、4カ月に一度移動する。ワーカーはラップトップを抱えてオフィス内を自由に移動できるが、ランチはキッチンで。「ここは私たちの『ホーム』。電子レンジ、ストーブ、冷蔵庫があり、みんなで一緒に話をしながらランチを食べています。自分のデスクで食事をしてはいけないというルールはないですが、できるだけみんなと食べるように勧めています。また、上階のカフェでは外部イベントが開かれることがあり、そうした場合にもこのキッチンがみんなの居場所になります」（同氏）

サステナビリティのために掃除には化学薬品を使わず、電解水を使う。自転車で通勤するワーカー向けにはシャワー付きでユニセックスの更衣室をつくった。いつでも運動できるようにとヨガやピラティスなど体を動かせるスペースもある。

テクノロジーについてはどうだろう。「テクノロジーはツールであり、結果ではありません。レセプションも実際に人間が受付をしていて、大きい

モニターなどがあるわけではありませんし、実際に人間味があってほしいと思っています。例えば、ビルの入退室からロッカーの施錠までを1つのカードで可能にすることで、よりシームレスなエクスペリエンスを実現させることができる。ロッカーを電子ロックにすることで、今後11年間はキーの管理をせずに済みます。データも見えるので、もし誰かが6カ月ロッカーを使っていなかったらまだ必要か確認できますし、来客に1週間貸すこともできる。テクノロジーを通してオペレーションを改善することができるのです」（同氏）

以上すべてが従業員の働き方を考慮に入れて決められた。「かかったのは大きな金額ではないですが、みんなに大きな影響を与えています」とマッキントッシュ氏は胸を張る。おかげで評判は上々。移転3カ月後の調査では、ワーカーの98%が「満足」と答えたという。移転当時453人だったワーカーが1年で520人まで増えたという事実も、新オフィスの成功を証明するに十分だ。

数々のデザイン賞に加え、アラップのメルボルン・オフィスはグリーンスターの6つ星を獲得している。さらに、WELL認証の新たな評価基準であるWELL v2のプラチナ認証を受けたオフィスの1つに輝いた。これはオーストラリアのみならず、世界で初めての快挙である。**WS**

最上階からGF（地上階）のキッチンスペースを望む。自然光の取り込みはもちろん、オフィス内の照明はサーカディアンリズム（概日リズム）を再現したシステムを導入し、ウェルネス向上を狙っている。

すべてのフロア、チームが視覚的につながり、より良いコミュニケーションに寄与している。「電話やメールを使うことなく、スタッフは簡単に顔を合わせることができます」（マッキントッシュ氏）

ERA-co
ユーザー・ストラテジー部門
グローバル・ディレクター
ジェームス・カルダー

James Calder
Global Director
User Strategy
ERA-co

大学卒業後、設計事務所ウッズバゴット
に入社。2012年にカルダー・コンサルタ
ンツを設立し、オーストラリアを中心に数々
のワークプレイス構築、チェンジマネジ
メントを手がける。2019年11月、同社は
エクスペリエンス・コンサルティング・エ
ージェンシーERA-coへと改称。

FOCUS 1

カルチャーに基づいた
エクスペリエンスをデザインする

James Calder

Designing experiences
rooted in culture

1／カルダー氏がコンセプトワークを行った、現在メルボルンに建設中の「80 Collins Street」。メルボルンのビジネスと商業の中心であるコリンズ・ストリートに面している。2つのオフィスタワーと低層部の商業エリアから成る。

2／ウッズバゴットとともに同氏が新たに設立したコンサルティング会社「ERA-co」。オフィス構築にとどまらない、エクスペリエンスのあり方から企業の課題解決を支援。ニューヨーク、メルボルン、シドニー、ロンドン、上海に拠点を持つ。

組織はよりフレキシブルに、働く場所や時間を調整できるようになった。Zoomや Skypeなどの利用で遠隔勤務もしやすい。限定されたテクノロジーしか用いない古いビジネスモデルは衰退していく。カルダー・コンサルタンツを通してオーストラリア含め世界中のワークプレイスのコンサルティングを行ってきたジェームス・カルダー氏は「（オーストラリアは）ほかの国々とおおむね同じトレンドをたどっている」と見ている。

空間プランニングにおいて、それは「多様性」として表れている。100％クローズドなオフィスではなく、100％オープンなプランでもなく、そのハイブリッド。

「企業によっては誰も自分のデスクを持ってはいけないということにしていますが、別の企業では個人のデスクはあったほうがいいとしています。さまざまな考えがあり、必ずしもABWにしなければならないわけでもありません。ハイブリッドは多くの企業にとっていいことだと私は思います」

ユーザー・エクスペリエンス重視の流れも顕著だ。まだ完全ではないにしろ、スペースの予約や飲食、ロッカーの使用に関するシステムへのコネクションをコントロールできる日は近い。だがカルダー氏は「ユーザー・エクスペリエンスの前に組織の価値観やカルチャーが重要」と指摘する。

人間は同じ性格、同じ目標を持つ者と同じグループに属することを好む。古いカルチャーに属していれば、古いオフィスから抜け出せないのが道理だ。逆に、一部のテクノロジー系企業のように、普段着で働き、ビールや食べ物を置いたオフィスで働くのも「単にそれが彼らのカルチャーだから」。Tシャツを着るのはTシャツが好きだから。ビールと食べ物を置いているのも長時間働く上で、買い物など余計な時間を使いたくないから。働き方とはつまり、カルチャーの表現なのだ。

となると、外部の人間たるビルのオーナーがこのようなユーザー・エクスペリエンスを提供するのは難しい。

「だからこそ企業が独自でしっかりマネジメント

しなければならないのです。People and Culture やファシリティ・マネジメント、テクノロジーの部署の人たちは、これからは共に企業のカルチャーに焦点を当てていく必要があります」

カルダー氏は昨年カルダー・コンサルタンツを「ERA-co」に改称し、コンサルティング・ソリューションをアップデートした。建築設計事務所ウッズバゴットのスポンサーのもと、文化人類学者やビジネス・アナリスト、データ・サイエンティストらが集まり、ワークプレイスのコンサルティングのみならず、ブランディングなど企業が抱えるより大きな問題に取り組んでいくという。カルダー氏が手がける未来のオフィスはどのようなものになっていくのだろう。

「今後は、ただのオフィスビルをつくっていくことはないと思います。従来のオフィスビルが減少傾向にあるのに対し、シェアスペース、ミーティングスペース、飲食やライフスタイルとワークスタイルを兼ね備えた空間が増加傾向にあります。ほかに変化しているのは、テナントビジネスのダイナミズムです。長期でリース契約をしなくなってきている。10年先に必要なスペースまで見越すことは不可能とも言えます。現在行っているリースの多くは柔軟性があり、そのような中心となるスペース、フレキシブルなスペース、そしてシェアスペースが欲しいという要望に応えるものです」

またテクノロジーにより遠隔でも「つながる」環境が整ったこと、また「つながる」ことを好む若者世代の登場も、オフィスを変えていく。「賃貸の借用という形から遠ざかり、代わりにビジネスコミュニティに変化していくと思います。そこで、ビルの中にさまざまなグループの業種のエコシステムを生み出すネットワークをつくっています」

デジタルとフィジカルの行き来も、よりシームレスになるだろう。カルチャーがエクスペリエンスとフィジカルに影響し、さらにデジタル・エクスペリエンスにも影響を及ぼしていく。

「ERA-coが、ソフトウェア・デベロッパーやデータ・サイエンティスト、ビル内にIoTをつなげられる人に投資したのはそのような理由からです。今はサービス系の会社とも話をしているところです。おそらく今後は、すべてのビルのシステムは遠隔からクラウドなどでマネジメントされることになると思います。さらに効率性やサステナビリティのマネジメント、またエクスペリエンスについて今よりずっといいデータを得ることができるでしょう。個々のビルだけではなく全体のデータがあるからです。結果、フィジカルにもバーチャルにも、より一体化したユーザー・エクスペリエンスになると思います。また、ビルのシステムもより生産的に運営されるでしょう。例えば飛行機のように、エンジンは航空会社ではなくGEかロールスロイスがつくり、クラウドでマネージしていく。いずれ、ビルもそうなると思います」

ビルがクラウドベースになるとは、どういうことか。

「企業は照明や空調、インフォメーション、エレベーターなどをまとめる。エレベーターはエレベーター会社が所有する。ビルのオーナーはそれに対して支払う。今の多くのシステムは間違ったものを測っていると思います。役立つデバイスはありますが、それでどうすればいいか、まだ答えを出せていない状態です。例えば、部屋の利用状況を測ることはできても質については教えてくれません。いいアプリも出ていて、SNSの視点からつくられたものなどがあり、いずれもとてもいいものですが、まだビルにつなげることはできていない。これからさまざまなことを1つの統合されたシステムにしていかなければいけないという状態です。それができるまでにこれから5年、10年かかると思います。難しいのは、ビルをコントロールしている人たちです。例えばファシリティ・マネジメントをコントロールする大きな不動産会社は元から革新的なタイプではなく、保守的なタイプの企業です。業界としてイノベーションに対するシステムがないのだと思います」

カルダー氏がERA-coでやりたいことの1つは、そこにある。テクノロジー系企業は新しい働き方やオフィスにおける問題をよく知らず、テナントやクライアントはこれらに興味はあっても、テクノロジーに特化していない。

「この1年ほど、会社のテクノロジーグループと仕事をするのではなく、外部からテクノロジー担当を連れてくるということを始めています。それが問題解決の初めの一歩だと思います」 **WS**

3／こちらも「80 Collins Street」（4、5も同様）。湾曲したファサードには照明が仕込まれ、夜間は「ストリートのランタン」として街をやさしく照らす。独自のポータルサイトがあり、入居企業は、さまざまなコンシェルジュサービスを受けることができる。

4／ビルの足元にはビクトリア様式の歴史的建造物を保存し、これらがストリートの景観を維持している。オフィスタワー（延床面積4万3,000㎡）、写真のロビーのほか、フードホール、ビジネスラウンジ、ホテル、ショッピングモールなどが広がる。

5／周辺から石畳を内部まで引き込むことでメルボルンらしいヒューマンスケールな路地裏空間を実現する。目抜き通りらしく、ブランドショップ、高級レストランが路面店に入る予定だ。

3

4

ボーウェン・ストリートのキャンパス中央部。ストリートとキャンパスの境目がなく、行き交う人々も学生と市民が入り交じる。ストリート・ファニチャーも開放されている。

CASE 6

街に開かれ、市民に開かれた
都市型キャンパス

RMIT University
［アールエムアイティー・ユニバーシティ］

An urban campus
open to the people of the city

メ　ルボルン中心部にメインキャンパスを置く
RMITユニバーシティ（ロイヤルメルボル
ン工科大学）。都市型キャンパスといえば聞こえ
はいいが、以前のキャンパスは街の一等地を専有
しながらストリートを背にし、閉鎖的だった。街
の活気から隔絶され、また大学も街に貢献するこ
となく無秩序に開発を重ねた。「街とキャンパス
の関係性を変える必要がありました」とRMITの
キャンパス・プランニング・サービス部門で働くニ
コール・イートン氏は話す。
　「ニュー・アカデミック・ストリート（New Academic
Street／NAS）」と名付けられた再生プロジェク
トは、閉じていたキャンパスを街に開くことが狙い
の1つだった。ソリューションはシンプルだ。市
民が行き来できるよう門を開放、キャンパスや施

設内に新しく道を通しリテールや公共スペースを
用意した。脇のベンチには学生と市民が隣り合う
形で座り、見分けがつかない。市民が利用できる
公共スペースが設けられ、街のにぎわいが昼夜を
問わずキャンパス内に流れ込む。
　外との関係だけではない。内側の空間も大きく
変化させ、学生たちにとっても、新しいキャンパ
スはすこぶる居心地がよいものになった。「いか
にスティッキー（粘着力のある）なキャンパスにす
るかという挑戦」（イートン氏）がなされたからだ。
　かつてRMITの学生は、授業が終わると街に出
ざるを得なかった。オーストラリアの大学には日
本の大学のようなゼミやラボがなく、学生の居場
所が限られる。「学生が好きに入って、カバンを
置いてお昼を買いに行ったり、授業に出てから戻

メイン校舎を横断するアーケード。2つの通りをつなぎ、学生だけでなく市民も自由に行き来する。大学を街に開こうとしたキャンパスの象徴的風景だ。

RMIT University
メルボルン
設立：1887年
学生数：8万6,839人（2018年）

1

2

ってくる、みたいな場所がないのです」（設計を務めたNMBWアーキテクチャー・スタジオのディレクター、マリカ・ネウストプニー氏）。そのため街のフードコートやモールに行ったきり帰らず、午後の授業をさぼる学生も少なくなかったという。NASプロジェクトの課題は、学生たちが一日中過ごせる環境をつくることだった。

「私たちが提供したのは、1人で座って勉強したり、グループで話をしたりできる場所です。今では、このキャンパスで自分の時間を過ごす学生がたくさんいます。特に街の中心に住む学生はそうですね。学生が住むアパートはたいてい狭くて、ベッドとデスク、バスルームがあるだけのようなところです。キャンパスに来れば、ここが彼らのリビングルームになります。夜10時過ぎまで学生が過ごすことも珍しくありません」（イートン氏）

設計にあたった建築家は、RMITユニバーシティのケリー・ライオン教授と、教授の元教え子4人。NMBWアーキテクチャー・スタジオのディレクター、ナイジェル・バートラム氏もその1人だ。以前のキャンパスは1人の建築家の手で設計され、建物は単一的で統一されていた。しかし今回はライオン教授の率いる建築設計事務所ライオンズが描いたマスタープランのもと、12棟の建物を5人が別々に設計することに。「このブロック自体を街のように」仕上げ、またセキュリティのため隠れ

るところはなく「どの建物からもほかの建物が見える」ヴィジビリティ（視認性）の高い空間とした。

テクノロジー面では、キャンパスのナビゲーション・アプリを開発したことが成果だ。まだプロトタイプだが、ボタン1つで警備員を呼べる機能、キャンパス外へのバスサービスの案内、自習室や資料の予約機能など、学生が必要とする情報がすべてアプリ内で手に入る。

今や、いつでもキャンパスに学生の姿がある。「金曜日の午後5時にも学生がたくさんキャンパスにいるのを見て『彼らはいったい、何をしてるんだろう?』と思ったこともありましたが、彼らは必ずしも勉強しているというわけではなく、キャンパスをただ利用しているんですね」（イートン氏）。狙い通り、まさしくスティッキーなキャンパスの完成だ。同氏は続ける。「最近はメルボルン大学の学生がここに来て過ごすこともあります」

この計画には続きがある。RMITとメルボルン大学2つの大学を結び、エリア一帯をイノベーションの基地とする「メルボルン・イノベーション・ディストリクト構想」だ。現時点ではプランニングの段階に過ぎないが、実現すれば「RMITユニバーシティは変わった」とさらに強く印象付けるものになるだろう。かつて文字通り街に背を向けていたRMITユニバーシティが、街に影響を与える存在になろうとしているのだ。 WS

1／学生がプロジェクトワークを行うエリア。設計は5つの建築事務所が手がけており、エリアによってデザインのテイストが全く異なる。多様な空間が学習意欲を刺激する。

2／ワークラウンジ。個人での作業や複数人が集まってのプロジェクトワークに利用されるスペース。リラックスできるようにロッキングチェアが多数置かれている。

3／キャンパス内の路地。飲食店とともに脇にはちょっとした作業や待ち合わせに使えるカウンターデスクが。こうした場所が「スティッキー」な効果を生む。

4／飲食店。パブリックスペースを増やす工夫として、テナントとして店舗に貸すのはキッチンまわりだけ。それ以外のテーブル席は店舗でドリンクを買わなくても自由に使える。

5／学生生活に関する各種サービスをワンストップで提供する「RMITコネクト」。都市型キャンパスで通学時間もかかる忙しい学生のためにクイックかつ的確にサポートするための仕組みが充実している。

ストリートに対して開かれた構造に

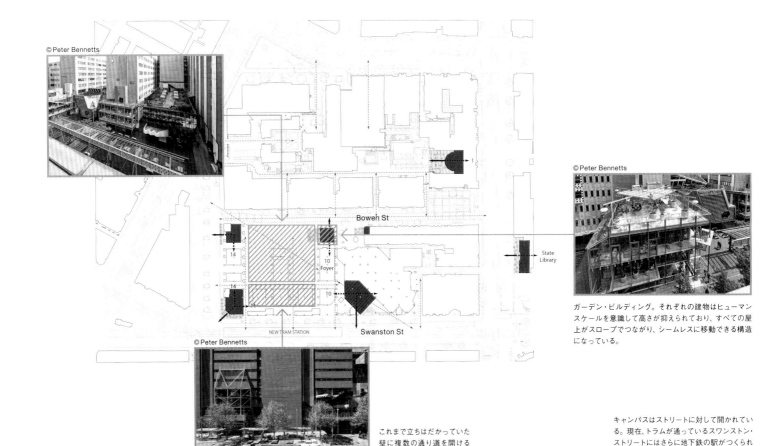

©Peter Bennetts

ガーデン・ビルディング。それぞれの建物はヒューマンスケールを意識して高さが抑えられており、すべての屋上がスロープでつながり、シームレスに移動できる構造になっている。

これまで立ちはだかっていた壁に複数の通り道を開けることで、街の活気がキャンパス内に入り込むようになった。

キャンパスはストリートに対して開かれている。現在、トラムが通っているスワンストン・ストリートにはさらに地下鉄の駅がつくられることになっており、今後は市民のキャンパス利用が飛躍的に増加することが予想される。

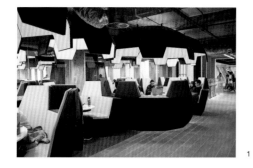

1

2

3

4

5

学生にも目に見える変化が

10,000+
STUDENTS

NASプログラムに参加した
学生数が1万人を超えた

80+
BUSINESSES

ポップアップ・ショップに展示
された、学生と卒業生による
ビジネスの件数が80を超えた

54
EVENTS

学生が主体となって企画した
イベントが54件開催された

キャンパスが新しくなってからの学生へ
の調査結果の一部。これらの数字からは、
学生の積極性や大学への関心が高まっ
たことをうかがい知ることができる。

RMITユニバーシティ
キャンパス・プランニング・アンド・
サービス
ニコール・イートン

Nicole Eaton
Campus Planning and Services
RMIT University

NMBWアーキテクチャー・スタジオ
ディレクター
ナイジェル・バートラム

Nigel Bertram
Director
NMBW Architecture Studio

NMBWアーキテクチャー・スタジオ
ディレクター
マリカ・ネウストプニー

Marika Neustupny
Director
NMBW Architecture Studio

オーストラリアの玄関口に新たなコミュニティを生む
バーティカル・ビレッジ

Quay Quarter Tower

［キー・クォーター・タワー］

Photo: AMP Capital

**A vertical village creates a new community
on Australia's doorstep**

キー・クォーター・タワーの外観。5層のボリュームが少しずつズレながら積み重なることで地域への威圧感を抑えながら、入居者には眺望とテラスを提供することができる。

1

2

1／オフィスフロア。5層それぞれ
のボリュームには大きなアトリウム
と螺旋階段が備わり、フロア間の
視認性を高めコミュニケーション
を誘発する。デロイトとAMPの入
居が予定されており、他社向けには、
限られた数のリース可能なスペー
スがある。

2／低層階のリテール側のエントラ
ンス。ワークとレジャーのミックス
を重要視する若い世代に向けて、
ライフスタイルやウェルビーイング
を意識した施設やレストランなど
をテナントとして募集している。

1／キー・クォーター・タワーが建つ
サーキュラー・キーの街並み。シド
ニーの中でも古くから文化施設の
集積地、金融を中心としたCBDと
して栄えている場所だ。埠頭の先
にはオペラハウスが見える。

2／各層にはテラスがある。こうし
たセミパブリックのコモンエリアが
あることで、偶然の出会いやコミュ
ニティ意識を醸成する。これも5
層をツイストしたことによる恩恵で
ある。

3／キー・クォーター・タワーには
市民が自由にアクセスできる庭園
があり、ここではパブリックアート
や眺望を楽しむことができる。

Quay Quarter Tower
シドニー
デベロッパー：AMPキャピタル
竣工：2022年
延床面積：10万2,000㎡

シドニー湾に面するサーキュラー・キーは、ヨーロッパからの開拓移住団がオーストラリアで最初に到着した地。周囲にはオペラハウス、アートギャラリー、博物館など数々の文化・芸術施設が点在し、古い金融街もある。つまりシドニーにとっては歴史的、文化的に貴重なエリア。しかし「ここ何十年も何の変化もなく、全体的に古く落ちぶれた雰囲気を醸し出していました」とAMPキャピタルのデベロップメント・ディレクター、マイケル・ウィートリー氏は言う。

進行中の再開発プロジェクトは、サーキュラー・キーの良さを残しながら活気ある街としてリニューアルしようというもの。この土地を60年以上所有するAMPキャピタルがデベロッパーである。まず動いたのは、シドニー市からの開発許可を取ることだった。それには周辺の歴史的な建造物

に日陰を落とすような悪影響を及ぼさずに開発を行う必要がある。

「そこでシドニー市とは、1970年に建てられたもともとの建物のコアの68%を利用してそのまま残し、周辺の景観には悪影響を及ぼさないようにする方針で合意しました」(ウィートリー氏)

ビルの名前は「Quay Quarter Tower(キー・クォーター・タワー)」。外観を見ての通り、5つのボリュームを積み重ねた「バーティカル・ビレッジ」がコンセプトで、村のようなコミュニティ感覚をビル全体でつくろうという意欲的なものになっている。それぞれの層はアトリウムと階段でつながれ、テナント企業のコミュニケーションと一体感を高める。5つの層を少しずつツイストさせながら重ねたのは、高層部に対しては、眺望の変化と各ボリュームの屋上にテラスを設け、低層部の地域に

対しては威圧感を抑えるため。市民が自由に楽しめるパブリックスペースを十分に確保するようにも配慮され、ビルの東西南北がつながるよう路地や遊歩道をつくり、人の往来を促している。完成予定は2022年。こうしたテナントや地域へのコミュニティ意識は市場に好意的に受け止められ、すでにAMP本社やデロイトのオーストラリア支社など、総面積の75%にあたるテナントが決まっている。

過熱するテクノロジーのムーブメントについてはどうだろう。「人はやはり、すでに存在するアプリ、慣れ親しんだアプリを使うことを好みますよね」とウィートリー氏。続けて、「英語に『白い象をつくり出す』という言い回しがあります。巨大なものをつくったものの、時間が経てば何の役にも立たないという意味です。アプリは柔軟で、すでに日常の一部であるもののほうがシームレスに使用

されます」と言う。「現在使われているテクノロジーと同じものが2年後に使われているとは限りません。（ビルの）完成が近づいた頃に、将来的にアップグレードが可能な優れたテクノロジーを取り入れていきたいと思います。テクノロジーの変化のスピードは建築業界のスピードとは全く違います。それが理由で、今までそれらをうまく合わせることに成功した人はいません」と、最新のビルでありながらテクノロジーに対する姿勢はいたって慎重である。

環境配慮の方針も抜かりはない。企業の環境負荷を評価するグリーンスターにおいて、ビルデザインで最高レベルの「6」を獲得している。一方、ビルのオペレーションについては評価が一段落ちる「5.5」だが、彼らにそれを気に留めている様子は全く見られない。フォーカスしているのは、環境よりもまず「人」だからだ。

「例えばハーブガーデンをつくれば、グリーンスターには認めてもらえるかもしれませんが、コミュニティの場としては全く意味を成しません」（ウィートリー氏）

キー・クォーター・タワーのシニア・デベロップメント・マネージャーを務めるブライアン・ドネリー氏が続ける。「私たちは階段やアトリウムなど、人が『使いたい』と思うスペースに投資することで、健康とウェルネスに対して、より純粋なアプローチを心がけています。階段はちょっとした運動になりますし、ほかの人とすれ違うこともできるので、交流を促進させる役目も果たします。会社にとっても、非常に重要なインフォーマルな情報交換の促進にもつながります。ですが、（そういったヒューマンサイドのアプローチは必ずしも）現在の評価ツールではポイントとは結び付かない。そういうことですね」 WS

ストリートからのアクセスも良好

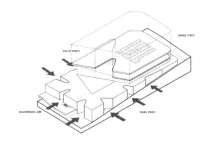

ポディウムと呼ばれる低層部は、緑豊かな庭園、レストラン、リテールを備える。複数の通りに面するエントランスは中央のアトリウムスペースに視覚的につながり、その透過性によって歩行者の流れを促進する。

美しい眺望を多方面に確保

5つのボリュームを少しずつずらして積み上げることで、低層部は地域に広く開き、高層部は地域の威圧感を減らし、入居者に眺望と屋上庭園を提供する。単なるデザインではなく合理的に課題が解かれている。

古いビルの構造を残した設計

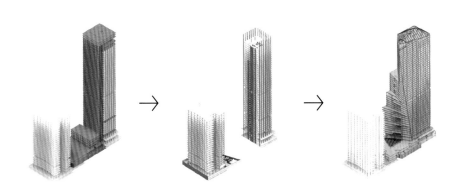

キー・クォーター・タワーは、1970年に建てられた古いビルの既存コアをアップサイクル。構造を68%残したままで新しいパーツを加えるというユニークな工法を採用することで、サステナビリティと工期短縮を実現する。コアに4つの新しいエレベーターシャフト、北側に約4万5,000㎡の新しい建築が追加される。

2

エーエムピー・キャピタル
デベロップメント・ディレクター、
キー・クォーター
マイケル・ウィートリー

Michael Wheatley
Development Director,
Quay Quarter
AMP Capital

キー・クォーター・タワー
シニア・デベロップメント・
マネージャー
ブライアン・ドネリー

Brian Donnelly
Senior Development Manager
Quay Quarter Tower

1／いわゆる「ライフスタイルエリア」と呼ばれるショッピングモール。活性化のための各種アクティビティ、イベントなどが計画されている。

2／写真右手がキー・クォーター・タワー。マンション、レストラン、ライフスタイルやウェルビーイング関連の店舗など、殺風景な旧来の金融街を美しく変化させるさまざまなリテールが並ぶ。

1

CASE 8

自社の革新性を体感してもらう
ショーケース

Mirvac

［マーバック］

**An experiential showcase of
one company's innovations**

Mirvac
シドニー
創業：1972年
従業員数：1,540人（2019年）

サ ウス・イヴリー（12ページ）をはじめ、革新的な不動産開発を手がけるマーバックにとって、本社オフィスが入るシドニーの「EYセンター」は自社の革新性をカスタマーに体感してもらうショーケースでもある。ビル6フロア分、7,000㎡を専有するオフィスのコンセプトが「フレキシビリティ」。固定デスク、ハイベンチ、コラボレーション・スペースなど多くのセッティングがあり、ワーカーはその日必要な働き方に合わせて選ぶことができる。在宅含め、社外での勤務もOKだ。「生産的で上司がパフォーマンスを好評価していれば

どこで働いてもいいことになっています」と同社のコマーシャル・デベロップメントでゼネラル・マネージャーを務めるサイモン・ヒーリー氏は言う。

もう1つ、マーバックのイノベーションに「ワークプレイス・ダイナミック・デンシティ（流動的密度）」がある。これは1つのワークステーションに何人を割り当てるかという考え方。アジャイル・ワークなどを理由にオフィスにいないワーカーの数を考えると、必ずしも1つのワークステーションに1人を割り当てる必要はない。この「ワークプレイス・ダイナミック・デンシティ」は大企業になるほど数

女性のチャリティ団体「YWCA NSW」が運営するカフェ。この団体からは賃料を取らず、カフェの利益はDVを撲滅するための同団体のサービスへの出資金として使われている。

72

字が高くなる傾向にあり、「当社では10のワークステーションに対し12人、つまり、（1つのワークステーションあたりでプラス）20％が標準的です」（ヒーリー氏）。ビル全体を見ても、オーストラリアで新規に建てられたオフィスビルの基準が「10〜12㎡に1人」であるところ、ここは8㎡に1人の密度になるよう設計されている。さらに、アジャイル・ワーク（オーストラリアではABWをこう呼ぶことが多い）によって流動的に人口密度は変化する。マーバックの従業員満足度を調べたデータを見ると、生産性は35％向上、視覚的な美しさは前オフィスの30％から91％へと改善。また「職場が健康にプラスの影響を与える」という認識も33％から88％へと向上した。

ビル設計にあたっては6つの建築事務所にコンセプトデザインを依頼した。「オフィスビルは一般的に矩形でデザインされますが、四角い形、ガラス、コンクリート、光が反射するという要素は特徴がなく、温かみに欠けます。それでも商業ビルですから、オフィスビルでありながらテナントを入れることができ、かつ新しさを感じるものにしてほしいと指示しました」とヒーリー氏は言う。コンペで採用されたのはシドニーの建築事務所FJMTによるもの。曲線的で木材を活用する設計はマーバックを満足させた。中でもトリプル・グレイズド・ファサード・システムは野心的だ。3層

1／シドニーのジョージ・ストリート200番地に建つビル「EYセンター」。マーバックがビルの開発を担当し、26Fから31Fの6フロアをオフィスとして占有。曲線的なフォルムと木材の質感が特徴だ。

2／3層のガラスからなる「トリプル・グレイズド・ファサード・システム」を採用。この木製ブラインドが、ビル全体の外観に優しい雰囲気を醸し出す。近づくと木目の表情の違いに気付く。

のガラスを持つ外装システムで太陽光線を遮り、3層の間にある密閉空間に木製のベネチアン・ブラインドを取り付ける。これがビル内外に木材の温かみを伝えるものになった。

マーバックはオフィス市場の今後をどう予測するだろう。その1つのトレンドがオフィス回帰だ。「どこでも働ける」環境が整備される一方で、オフィスで働く意味が顕在化された。コラボレーションやカルチャー醸成には、人が集まるオフィスがやはり有効と多くの企業が考え始めている。

「企業にとってオフィスは企業カルチャーや帰属意識などの面で重要です。『誰もがリモートワークを求めている』という考えもありましたが、実のところ多くの企業では、人は対面で仕事をすることや人とのつながりを持つことを好んでいることに気付いています」(ヒーリー氏)

オフィスビルにパブリックスペースやリテールスペースを設けるトレンドにも同じ理由がある。そして、オーストラリアの企業の多くが、デザインやアートワークを通じて国の伝統や先住民の文化を尊重することにも。

「それはビルのヒューマニスティックな側面です。みなパブリックアートを見に行くのが好きで、歴史の片鱗を見ることや、それを自身でクリエイティブに解釈することを好みます。新しくつくるビルにはこれまで以上にそうした要素を取り入れていきます。テナントに対しては、リテールやパブリックアートはどんなものか、文化的意義はどうなのか、ビルにソウル(魂)はあるのか、ビルに入ったときにいい気持ちになるのか、そうした要素を求めますし、今後ますます重要になるでしょう」(ヒーリー氏) WS

マーバック
コマーシャル・デベロップメント
ゼネラル・マネージャー
サイモン・ヒーリー

Simon Healy
General Manager
Commercial Development
Mirvac

地上階のビル共用エントランス。快適で落ち着ける家具を揃え、壁一面には先住民への敬意を表したアート。オフィスというよりはホテルの雰囲気を目指した。

1

1／マーバックが占有する6フロアはフロア中央に内部階段を設け、社員の交流を活性化している。顔認証セキュリティも採用し、社員のスムーズな動きを阻害しない。

2／階段の終着点にはコミュニケーションを誘発するハブが必ず用意されている。トレーニングセンターやキッチンも併設され、社員間の偶然の出会いをさらに加速する。

3／アジャイルワークを採用しているため、ワーカーは自分の働く時間と場所を自由に選択することができる。囲われ感のあるコンセントレーションブースが人気だ。

4／執務室内の通路上に配置された細長いキッチン。往来の多さが偶然の出会いを誘発する。ここはタッチダウン的な作業スペースとしても機能している。

3

2

4

FOCUS 2

「スーパー・エクスペリエンス」が
未来のワークプレイスを変える

Super-Experience

Changing the future of workplaces
through super-experiences

マーバック
ワークプレイス・エクスペリエンス
ゼネラル・マネージャー
ポール・エドワーズ

Paul Edwards
General Manager
Workplace Experiences
Mirvac

マーバックに勤務し、ワークプレイス研
究の権威ジェレミー・マイヤーソン氏が
率いるワークテック・アカデミーと共同で
スーパー・エクスペリエンスの研究を手
がける。2019年2月、『スーパー・エクス
ペリエンス – デジタル・ワークプレイス
における人材のためのデザイン』を発表。

今日のグローバル・デジタルエコノミーにおいて、企業は優れた職場体験を提供し、優秀な人材を惹き付け維持し、イノベーションとクリエイティビティを促進することは自明だ。それが、マーバックが提供するオフィスにおいて「スーパー・エクスペリエンス」を重視する理由である。これを理解するにはリテールの変遷を知るのが近道だ。

15年以上前にアマゾンが誕生して以来、リテール事業者は「なぜショッピングセンターがあるのか」と問い、「顧客はアマゾンに代替されないエクスペリエンス（体験）が欲しいからだ」という結論にたどり着いた。それこそアマゾンに代替されない価値だからだ。そのようにして、事業者はリテールをエクスペリエンスと結び付けようとしてきた。フードコートはダイニングセンターになり、ボーリング場や映画館がショッピングセンターに拡張された。「ただハンバーガーを食べるのではなく、いいレストランでシャンパンを飲み、いい食事をしてから買い物をするのです」とポール・エドワーズ氏は言う。それがエクスペリエンスとリテールを結び付けるということだ。

同じようにエクスペリエンスとワークプレイスを結び付けるにはどうすべきか？

「オーストラリアでは、2024年にはベビーブーム世代からデジタルに強いミレニアル世代へと大勢が入れ替わります。テクノロジーの急速な発展に伴い、これまでのワークプレイスが一変することは間違いないでしょう。人々は新しいスキルを継続的に学ばなくてはならなくなります。そのように学習する人々を支えるため、ラーニング・エクスペリエンスをいかにして創出できるかを私たちは考えています」

マーバックは、そのような「日常のエクスペリエンス」だけではなく、スーパー・エクスペリエンスを研究し始めた。それはクリエイティビティや感情に影響を与える超越した体験の総称だ。

「私たちが考えるスーパー・エクスペリエンスとは、ドラマティックであり、『わお！　すごい！』と思うようなエクスペリエンスです」。こうしたインスピレーションを与えることが、ワーカーが新しい考え方や創造性を発揮することにつながっていくのだ。

「スーパー・エクスペリエンスをつくる3つのキー・ファクターがあります。Awe（畏れ、畏敬）インスパイアリング、キュレーテッド、ラーニングです。ロジカルスタンダードなエクスペリエンスから感情やクリエイティブなエクスペリエンスに移行できれば、仕事に新しい興味が湧いてきます」

彼らはどのようにスーパー・エクスペリエンスをつくっているのだろう？　クライアントの目標、解決したい問題、「オフィスにいたい」と思わせるエクスペリエンスは何か、逆にそう思うことを阻害するエクスペリエンスは何か。例えば、ゲストがEYセンターのマーバック本社オフィスに入る際のエクスペリエンスを、彼らはこのように改善した。

「以前はフロントに着いたら、まず列に並ぶことになる。フロントが来客の用件を知るまでに時間がかかるわけです。このプロセスを簡素化するため、フロントが取るべき対応を調査しました。そして、ゲストが到着前に訪問相手に対してメールを送ることができるシステムを開発しました。このシステムによってアクセスにかかる時間をかなり削減することができ、ゲストのエクスペリエンスは大幅に改善されたのです」

「将来的には、来客がオフィスから100m以内に近づいたら私にメッセージが通知され、ゲストを乗せたエレベーターがどの階に向かっているかも自動的にわかるようになるでしょう。でも、人間の温かみ、フレンドリーさも要素としては非常に重要です。すべてをテクノロジーの視点から考えてはいけない。レセプションには、ゲストを歓迎するコンシェルジュもいますから」

マーバックでは、自社オフィスだけでなく、オーストラリア中の商業ビルにおいてもスーパー・エクスペリエンスの設計に寄与している。都市でうまく活用されていない土地を農園に転換すること、インタラクティブなアートワークをロビーで展開することもそう。マーバックが主導して進めたソリューションの1つである。 WS

スーパー・エクスペリエンスの生まれる領域

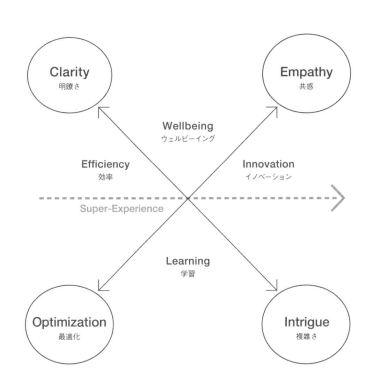

スーパー・エクスペリエンスの概念図。エクスペリエンスが明瞭さ、最適化の領域から複雑さ、共感の領域に移行するにつれて、スーパー・エクスペリエンスが出現する。

マーバックが所有するフレキシブル・オフィス「Hoist」。スーパー・エクスペリエンスを感じさせるホスピタリティだ。

スペースを活用するため、本社オフィスの駐車場を農園に改修。ストレス解消につながり、ワーカーの94%が幸せと回答したという。

WRAP-UP

テクノロジーに「動員」される人間

テクノロジーは私たちの生活になくてはならない存在だ。スマートフォンを開けば自分に最適化された情報が提示され、買い物でも何でもできるような環境で日々生活をしている。作家・編集者のスチュアート・ブランドが提示する社会変化の構造「ペース・レイヤリング」に従えば、変化の最先端はファッションやコマースといったコンシューマーに近いところでまず起こる。その次に、企業や行政などのインフラやガバナンスといった層で起こる。現在、コンシューマー向けに展開される個人データをベースにした新しいテクノロジーの活用が、伝統的なホワイトカラーの職場にまで忍び寄ってきている。

すでにギグエコノミーと呼ばれる短期的な労働市場においては、文化人類学者アレックス・ローゼンブラットが『Uberland ウーバーランド ——アルゴリズムはいかに働き方を変えているか——』で描写するように、アルゴリズムが労働者を直接し、厳密なマネジメント下に置い

人を助けるはずのテクノロジーがなぜ人を疎外するのか。哲学者マルティン・ハイデガーは、産業革命以降の近代的なテクノロジーの持つ特性を「総動員立て体制（Gestell）」と呼び、それを生み出した人間の意図を超えて、ただひたすらに自然エネルギーを効率的に使うという有用性のためだけに機能するとした。ギグエコノミーの現状が指し示すものは、まさに人間も1つの「自然エネルギー」としていかに使えるのか、有用性という意味においてテクノロジーに動員されているということだろう。

分散化が「感情の劣化」を引き起こす

ウーバーのように労働者がアルゴリズムで直接支配される世界は、人間が想像できる因果ではなく期間によって物事が決められており、なぜそのような指示になるのか意味を見出せない無意味感や労働だけが残っていく。「ワーカー」は人間の尊厳を失い、誰かに管理される

長期以降、生まれ育った地方を離れて都心への大量移住によって労働力が供給されてきたため、企業は地域社会に代わる共同体であったと言えよう。しかし組織の拡大に伴いコミュニティの規範を保つことが難しくなり、成果主義、派遣労働者など、規範の代わりにワーカー間での競争や代替可能な労働力を使って組織が運営されるようになると共同体意識はさらに薄れていった。そこにさらにテクノロジーが分散的な労働（ABW）を実現し、一気に組織の希薄化が進んだ。

一方で、ABWのような時間と場所に制約を持たない働き方は、労働人口が減少する先進国においては至上命題であるフレキシビリティを高めることに大いに効果を発揮する。

しかし、個別性の高いワーカーの動きが前提となるにつれ、マネージャーを介しての人的な管理手法は難しくなり、位置情報や作業情報などデータワークを把握するような動きが加速し、そこにテクノロジーの介在が常態化すると

テクノロジーに隙を見せないためには？
「感情の劣化」を防ぐオーストラリアの実践

本誌編集長 山下正太郎

分散型の働き方ABWとテクノロジーが融合するとき
個人がテクノロジーに隷属する未来が描かれやすい。
そこに抗うオーストラリアの実践とは？

会は共同体を弱め、孤独を引き起こし、全世界的な社会問題となっている。イギリスでは、孤独を現代の公衆衛生における最大の課題として、2018年に世界で初めて「孤独担当大臣」のポストを設けた。別の観点では、裁量労働と成果主義が組み合わさることにより、数値だけで評価され、それを挽回すべく長時間労働を助長する問題も指摘されている。行き過ぎたABWは共同体の空洞化や個人の疲弊を引き起こす。

グローバルに広がり、母体の大きくなった企業のガバナンスを考えるとき、テクノロジーを活用することは統治コストを下げる観点で避けられないように思われる。統治側のロジックでは、ある種のパターナリズムとして労働者を望ましい行動や幸福な状態に仕向けていくのでWin-Winの関係とするのだが、それもまた労働者が自覚なく隷属されている点で疑問が残る。一方、その統治になじまない人たちは功利主義的な文脈の中で、少数派の個人が捨てられるいわゆる「トロッコ問題（Trolley Problem）」に直面してしまう。

内包される場「コミュニティスタイル」

2000年代にいち早くオランダからABWを取り入れ、いまや世界最先端のトップランナーとして独自の世界を構築するオーストラリアは「感情の劣化」について今すぐ対応していそうに思える。問題事例を少し紐解いてみよう。

CBAでは、デジタルバンク・ナンバーワンを目指すために、今回の移転でテックタレントの知の集約を図った。ワーカーには極めてテクノロジーオリエンテッドなワークスタイルを実現するための環境が与えられているが、それ以前にまず重視したこと、それは「コミュニティ」だ。物語性を感じさせる地域にオフィスを構え、地域一帯の「良き隣人」であろうと地域貢献の場を設けた。さらにオフィス内部にも、コミュニティを支える場をふんだんに設けてテクノロジーに先行してワーカーの心のよりどころをデザインした。

パラマウント・ハウスは、同じポストコードを共有する人たちに対して、顔の見える「新たな教会」をつくろうとした。対象となったのは、デジタルネイティブであるミレニアル世代だ。ネイバーフッドに対してテクノロジーで何かを解決するのではなく、1つひとつ自分たちにとって意味あるテナントを吟味して豊かな生活環境をつくり上げた。路面に広かれたカフェでは、ネイバーズたちの語らいやビジネスミーティングなど生き生きとした世界が日々広がっている。

すべてをここに挙げられないが、今号の事例は、スマートテクノロジーをあくまでも手段と捉え、自分たちのより良い共同体をつくることを何よりも優先し、投資をしていた。

あわせて、自分が所属したいと思える地域より良い地域を創出する「プレイスメイキング」への意識も挙げたい。訪れる場は個人を歓迎的に...

で豊かな共通体験を生み出すことにつながる。共通体験とは、必ずしも集まった人たちが言葉を交わしたり、一緒に何か行動したりすることではない。その場に身を置くことで、みんながそこに「内包されている感覚」を持てるかどうかがポイントだ。内包され、少しでも共同体のメンバーのことに思いを馳せられるようになれば「感情の劣化」は防がれる。

今号の事例ではなかったが、テクノロジー側からそうした内包される場をつくる動きも見られる。例えば「プラットフォーム・コーポラティビズム」と言われる、共同組合をつくりテクノロジーを介してそれを運営していこうという取り組みだ。

こうした共同体をつくることを可能にする背景には、個々人の確固たる「意志」が必要であるということも指摘しておきたい。オーストラリアの場合は、世界的なライフスタイル大国としても知られているように、一人ひとりのワーカーにありたい人生のイメージがあるからこそ、支えたい、あるいはつくりたい共同体があるのだ。個々のライフスタイルを統合する形での「コミュニティスタイル」とも呼べるような行動様式がつくられている。

人々が最底を失ったとき、テクノロジーは我々の生活や仕事の思惑をかっさらってゆくことになるのだろう。オーストラリアにはそれを防ぐための社会が実装されている。人間はテクノロジーに隷従してはいけないのだ。（略）

山下正太郎
Shotaro Yamashita

コクヨ株式会社 ワークスタイル研究所 所長
次世代ワークプレイスの研究、コンサルティングに従事。2016〜2017年、英ロイヤル・カレッジ・オブ・アート ヘレン・ハムリン・センター・フォー・デザイン客員研究員。

DATA SHEET
[データシート]

CBA
コンサルティング（ワークスタイル）: 非公開
建築設計（ビル）: FJMT
インテリア設計: Woods Bagot
Consultancy for Work Style: N/A
Building Architect: FJMT
Interior Design: Woods Bagot

Paramount House
コンサルティング（ワークスタイル）: 非公開
建築設計: Right Angle Studio
インテリア設計: 非公開
Consultancy for Work Style: N/A
Architect: Right Angle Studio
Interior Design: N/A

Aurecon
コンサルティング（ワークスタイル）: 非公開
建築設計（ビル）: Bates Smart
インテリア設計: Woods Bagot
Consultancy for Work Style: N/A
Building Architect: Bates Smart
Interior Design: Woods Bagot

Woodside
コンサルティング（ワークスタイル）: Unispace
建築設計: Cox Architecture
インテリア設計: Unispace
Consultancy for Work Style: Unispace
Architect: Cox Architecture
Interior Design: Unispace

Arup
コンサルティング（ワークスタイル）:
Hassell partnered with Arup
建築設計: 非公開
インテリア設計: Hassell
Consultancy for Work Style: Hassell partnered with Arup
Architect: N/A
Interior Design: Hassell

RMIT University
コンサルティング（ワークスタイル）: 非公開
建築設計: Lyons with NMBW Architecture Studio,
Minifie van Schaik Architects,
Harrison and White, and Maddison Architects
インテリア設計: 非公開
Consultancy for Work Style: N/A
Architects: Lyons with NMBW Architecture Studio,
Minifie van Schaik Architects,
Harrison and White, and Maddison Architects
Interior Design: N/A

Quay Quarter Tower
コンサルティング（ワークスタイル）: 非公開
建築設計（ビル）: 3XN architects of Denmark and Australia
インテリア設計: Tom Dixon's Design Research Studio
Consultancy for Work Style: N/A
Architect: 3XN architects of Denmark and Australia
Interior Design: Tom Dixon's Design Research Studio

Mirvac
コンサルティング（ワークスタイル）: 非公開
建築設計: FJMT
インテリア設計: Davenport Campbell
Consultancy for Work Style: N/A
Architect: FJMT
Interior Design: Davenport Campbell

EDITORS' NOTE
[編集後記]

実に5年ぶりとなったオーストラリア取材。有袋類の進化と同じく、この地のワークスタイル／ワークプレイスもまた独自の姿を世に提示し続けている。何度も述べたように、原点にはワーカーたちにこうありたいという強いライフスタイルの意志があるからだ。街場のコーヒーがこんなにおいしい理由もよくわかる。（山下）

本号の取材を行った2019年10月時点、シドニーは住宅価格の高騰及び通勤事情の悪化に悩まされていた。ABWをはじめとする分散型のワークスタイルは推進せざるを得ない状況のようだ。ウェルビーイングに対する取り組み、ABW、スマートワークプレイスと、ここ数年で働く環境の変化が加速している。（金森）

It has been five years since we last covered Australia, and, much like the evolution of marsupials, the workstyle/workplace here continues to present its own unique form to the world. As I've said many times, at the root of this approach is a strong desire for workers to define the way they live. It's easy to see why street coffee tastes so good.
—— Shotaro Yamashita

At the time we visited for this issue of the magazine, in October 2019, Sydney was plagued by high real-estate prices and worsening commuting conditions. The situation seemed to call for a drive toward ABW and other decentralized workstyles. The commitments to wellbeing, ABW, and smart workplaces illustrate the accelerating changes in the country's working environment over the last few years.
—— Yuki Kanamori

次号予告に代えて

本誌編集長　山下正太郎

新型コロナウイルス（COVID-19）の世界的感染拡大に伴い、安全かつ円滑に海外取材を実施すること、また我々自身がウイルスの運び手になる可能性を払拭することが難しくなっています。大変残念ではありますが、状況が沈静化するまで新規の発刊を控える判断をいたしました。この世界的有事に対して一人ひとりが「地球市民」としてどうふるまうか、そこには媒体を通じて伝えてきた「新しい時代を切りひらく働き方のリテラシー」がきっと役に立てると思っています。読者の皆様とはそう遠くない未来に、こんなシリアスな文章が杞憂だったと笑い飛ばせるうちにお目にかかれることを期待して。どうぞご無事で。

In lieu of a preview of the next issue

Editor-in-Chief: Shotaro Yamashita

With the global spread of the new coronavirus (COVID-19), it has become difficult to conduct overseas coverage safely and smoothly, and to dispel the possibility that we may become carriers of the virus ourselves. It is with great regret that we have decided to refrain from publishing new issues until the situation calms. I am sure that our magazine's message of promoting "literacy in work styles for a new era" will be useful in determining how each of us should behave as "global citizens" in the face of this crisis. I hope that in the not-too-distant future readers will be able to laugh at the fact that this serious tone of writing was unwarranted. I hope you stay safe.

www.worksight.jp

CASE 1

CBA

Australia's largest mega-bank aims to be number one in digital through people power

CBA
Sydney
Established: 1911
Employees: 48,238 (2019)
Total assets: 976.5 billion AUD (2019)

Commonwealth Bank of Australia (CBA) is the largest bank in Australia, with over 48,000 employees. Their newest office, Axle, aims to consolidate locations across Sydney in the newly redeveloped district of South Eveleigh. As part of its strategy to "become the leading bank in digital," CBA sought to bring employees close together and encourage collaboration. Roughly 4,000 people already work in the new space, which has a total area of 43,000 square meters, including 6,000 square meters of offices on each floor. Combined with a new building opening across the street, approximately 10,000 CBA employees will work in the area.

At this size, CBA Axle is more like a city campus than a single office. "There was very much an aspiration to not only create an amazing building inside but to create an amazing precinct, essentially," said Bradhly Le, a Senior Associate at Woods Bagot, the design firm responsible for this workplace's design. South Eveleigh has an abundance of spaces open to the community, including a skatepark, a tennis court, a basketball court, and a treehouse. Proceeds from CBA's kitchen space are all donated to charity.

"We try to be good neighbors," says Lawrence Chan, an executive manager at CBA. Companies that are active in this kind of place-making are more appealing to young people, which contributes to CBA's ability to attract talent from the nearby Sydney and New South

The dynamic atrium is reminiscent of a vast valley. Offices surround the space on three sides, and natural light shines through the skylight. Increasing visibility allows the energy of the entire workplace to be felt.

Wales Universities. That young talent is, of course, the company's best asset as it seeks to become number one in the digital field.

"When they leave the office and they want to go to the gym, the medical center, or the shopping center, all those things are nearby. All of that plays into the consideration of a good workplace," Chan explains, suggesting that a workplace is more than just a place of work.

Let's take a look inside the building. The plaza on the ground floor is a central location where people, including workers from outside the company, naturally gather and collaborate. ABW encourages people to move and collaborate freely, but an open-plan design simply wasn't enough. One challenge is workers' individual personalities. How can a workplace elicit interaction from people who are introverted and not inclined toward collaboration? Places where individuals can work quietly and anonymously are necessary, especially when the surroundings are lively—it was important to design areas partitioned with curtains or

booths to create an emphasis on privacy.

There have been 2.5 stages in CBA's implementation of ABW. The first stage began seven or eight years ago, with a simple open office; the second stage saw open-workplace architecture fitted to accommodate various specific goals. However, these designs still did not bring out all workers' best performance, so this latest iteration has taken into account the characteristics of both introverts and extroverts.

"ABW has unlocked flexibility for the bank to enable that level of staff empowerment and engagement. Their ability to choose where they work and how they work consistently comes up in our staff surveys as the biggest benefit of working at CBA," says Chan.

The use of the latest technology is not very noticeable. As in many smart workplaces, reception and seat reservations are done through a proprietary app. In line with their mission to become a leading digital bank, CBA also provides workers with the best digital UX; the data is used to understand how efficiently

1. Cafeteria. Some dine, while others work on their laptops. The entire interior, not only the cafeteria, utilizes wood to create a warm tone. Over 3,800 plants fill the space.
2. A quiet space nestled behind the main entrance for employees to retreat for work or relaxation. It's a refinement of CBA's previous ABW space, which was a more open layout, supporting collaboration and movement.
3. Activity can be seen on each floor by looking over the stairwell. The structure allows you to visually sense the movement and presence of people, no matter where you are.
4. The plaza on the ground floor, as seen from upper levels, features spots that encourage interaction, such as a café and meeting rooms. Both guests and employees are invited to use these facilities.

4

1. The main area used by the facility team. In addition to basic desks, there are also elevated workstations. The large whiteboards also function as floor dividers. Eschewing mass-produced items, the furniture is mostly custom-made.

2. The theater space in the center of the office, featuring tiered seating. Events are held every day, bringing liveliness to the office. When we visited, a seminar on healthy eating was being held.

3. Both the design and lines of movement are streamlined. "Nature doesn't really do straight lines," says Le. This ceiling also incorporates a streamlined biophilic design, inspired by various plants and nature.

4. An app developed in-house at CBA manages building access and lockers around the building. Employees are able to scan a QR code to report any issues with the facilities, which enables more efficient facility management.

5. The location of each worker can be detected by tracking where they connect their PCs to LAN cables. The data is used to improve the number and location of facilities based on frequency of use.

Lawrence Chan
Executive Manager
Commercial Design &
Delivery Group
CBA

Bradhly Le
Senior Associate
Woods Bagot

South Eveleigh,
a new innovation district

South Eveleigh, a suburb of Sydney, was once home to a flourishing steam-locomotive factory—much of the infrastructure that modernized Australia was built here. After falling on hard times in recent years, the city is now being reimagined by the real-estate developer Mirvac (page 114) and a consortium of AMP Capital, Sunsuper and Centuria Property Funds, and is currently in the process of attracting more people as Australia's new innovation district. The area is also notable for tennis courts, farms, and other sports and recreational facilities open for people to enjoy. Eventually, nine commercial buildings will be completed, featuring a mix of supermarkets, beauty salons, gyms, and outdoor cafés. In homage to Sydney's Aboriginal Gadigal people, a central feature of the redeveloped area is its emphasis on connecting with the local community.

© Eberle Photography

Ground-floor plaza. The café stand is in the foreground, but there is no apparent boundary between it and the lounge and theater space. The aim is to encourage non-territorial movement.

the building is used and see how often facilities are accessed.

"The data allowed us to see spots on the floor that aren't being used," says Chan. "Maybe there's a broken desk and somebody's been avoiding it for six months but we don't know why. The heat map data will tell you that desk hasn't been used [and] something is wrong with it."

This is a campus for people to work freely and flexibly. It's a place for all generations, from Baby Boomers to Generation X and Millennials, and for workers with disabilities. In that sense, CBA is seeking a different kind of inclusiveness from that of other tech giants. Le says that a space designed "just to be cool for the Millennials" isn't what they are after.

Throughout the design process, thought was put into helping people adjust to the change. Some staff members were accustomed to having their own offices and workstations, and the change meant losing that. Providing regular updates on the workspace as plans unfolded helped ensure that no one felt left behind. This campus belongs to the community, and it belongs to all employees. WS

1. Office exterior. The area of each floor is roughly 6,000 square meters. "It's a bit larger than a football field," says Le.
2. New employees are given training after their first day to help them adapt to working in an ABW workplace.
3. A lounge space near the entrance. These communication spaces are concentrated near the ground floor in order to encourage collaboration between employees and guests.
4. A communication hub, called "Pergola," in the office area. This serves as a place for workers to connect over drinks and snacks.
5. Public spaces, including a skate park, line the building's perimeter. The neighborhood and office are connected by a boardwalk, enabling the connection between business and community.
6. The new building in South Eveleigh, set to be completed in 2021 (55,000m²). "It will be the largest or second largest in Australia," says Chan. Once completed, CBA's digital staff will move there, and a total of 10,000 workers will work between the new space and CBA Axle.

CASE 2

Paramount House

**A gathering place for the creative community
of postcode 2010**

Paramount House
Sydney
Opened: 2014

Surry Hills is a village tuned in to the latest trends, lined with cafés and curated shops. One of its landmarks is a row of buildings—formerly owned by Paramount Pictures and 20th Century Fox—that were considered icons of Australian film culture through the early 1970s. In the days before the internet, people passing by on the street would look up at the beautiful brick buildings and envision Hollywood glamour. However, more than thirty years after the two companies left the town, the tenants continued to struggle.

The once ill-fated building has since been revived as Paramount House, a mixed-use facility that fosters a local creative community, through the work of Right Angle Studios, the developer and consulting agency responsible for the new design. Reflecting on past businesses that failed to take root in the community, Right Angle was careful in choosing each new tenant: a café, a cinema, a bar, a sports club, and a co-working space. "This is quite unusual in Australia," says Barrie Barton, the director of Right Angle Studio. "Usually there is a big rush, so all the new tenants start at once."

The first tenant chosen was Paramount Coffee Project. Barton was convinced that serving quality coffee would create a new community and lead to a chain of success, because, as he says, "Surry Hills people drink coffee every day." Gauging a tenant's willingness to cooperate was also key. Many people create their own communities within

Paramount Coffee Project. In Australia, which has developed a unique café culture, it's not uncommon to see business people meeting over coffee in the morning.

On the rooftop floor there is the Paramount
Recreation Club which houses a café, a yoga
studio, and a massage room. The fitness club has
a membership system, but the café is accessible
to everyone.

Barrie Barton
Director
Right Angle Studio

Naomi Tosic
Founder
The Office Space

1. "We wanted to have the best quality [tenant] in each category," says Barton—a point of pride for him. The café is where people can spend time as they please, whether it's for relaxation or for work.
2. Near the entrance of the café. Most visitors are local residents who live a short walk away. Many Paramount House workers also live in the area. Mornings are usually full of business meetings.
3. The Paramount Coffee Project was the first tenant invited to Paramount House, followed by a movie theater, a bar, and an advertising company's workspace on the top floor. Paramount House is the heart of the local community.

the building, and Barton actively pursued businesses that were enthusiastic about sharing space and creating friendly relationships. The eight years it took to fill all the spaces has proved worth the trouble—each tenant has successfully integrated into the town.

Barton believes that Sydney's lack of public transportation makes it unfriendly to travelers, remarking that "there's no Yamanote line." People who visit Paramount House also tend to live nearby. These neighbors live in the same area as the building: postcode 2010. Surry Hills is one of the most densely populated areas in Australia, home to many young, single people who work in central Sydney, which is a mere five-minute walk away. They're always looking for new and interesting things to do, so it's only natural that they set their eyes on Paramount House. Companies like Paramount House—community oriented and with a strong sense of responsibility toward the local area—share values important to Millennials.

"The older generations, maybe fifty-five and older, are very different than the younger generation. The younger generations have always had the internet, and they understand the relationship between them and other people [as a] community, [whether through] Facebook or Instagram. They [want to] express their values [on] climate change [or] gay marriage." says Barton.

Millennials' values are reflected in each workspace. They aren't satisfied with just a place to work in. Naomi Tosic, the founder of The Office Space, the company responsible for the co-working space in Paramount House, describes coming to work as "the new church."

1. Paramount House Hotel, located within Paramount House. Of the twenty-nine guest rooms, no two have the same design. This room, called "Sunny," boasts French linen sheets, a terrazzo bathroom, and a plant-filled alcove.
2. Paramount House Hotel reception area. Works by artists from Australia are on display. Guests can choose sparkling water, kombucha, or beer at the taps by the counter.
3. Some of the hotel rooms have a small inner balcony. The louvers let in a dry breeze and natural light.
4. Paramount House signage. Modest and sophisticated graphics and signage are placed here and there—the aim is to fit in with the community, not stand out.

She says, "People want the spiritual and they want the community, […] so I think we're elevating to meet those needs." This generation is eager for human interaction, preferring movie theaters to Netflix and cafés over UberEats. The interior design is neutral and sophisticated so as not to interfere with those interactions.

Today, Right Angle Studio is receiving a steady stream of office-design requests from large corporations, which tend to be conservative and are looking for outside influences for new work environments that can attract younger people. "Our clients […] take advice from lots of different types of consultants. We are unusual consultants. We have learned through […] watching people in the building, a different way of thinking about what people need. We are just a very small niche advisor to them, but because we are small we can provide unexpected, brave, different ideas," says Barton. **WS**

5. Exterior of Paramount House seen in the far right of the image. The Art Deco building was previously the Australian headquarters of Paramount Pictures.

6. Poly wine bar, a tenant of Paramount House. They offer affordable food and drinks with a focus on Australian wines.

7. The workspace of an advertising company on the top floor of Paramount House. The atmosphere of the community was what attracted this firm to move in.

8. The Office Space, a co-working space. Twenty-two companies are based here today. Each has its own private space, while the shared space allows for interaction.

9. A movie theater, modeled after a 1930s screening room. Two films are screened a night, six days a week, and business presentations and workshops are held here during the day.

10. Golden Age Cinema & Bar, located inside the theater and operated by Right Angle Studio.

11. Paramount Recreation Club, a 24-hour fitness center. 220 classes are offered each week, including yoga and boxercise classes.

12. A private room within the co-working space. Workers mingle in the kitchen during teatime. Perhaps owing to the comfort of the space, the tenant lineup remains the same three years after opening.

Aurecon

One of the world's largest timber office buildings is a second home to workers

Aurecon
Brisbane
Established: 2009
Employees: Approximately 7,500 (2019)

1.6 kilometers from Brisbane's Central Business District, a massive redevelopment project called Showgrounds, by the development heavyweight Lendlease, is underway. Around the time the project was launched, the engineering, design, and advisory company Aurecon's lease on their CBD office was ending, and they were in the market for a new site for their 700 employees. They had worked with Lendlease on many projects in the past. For Aurecon, being able to collaborate on the design and construction of a timber skyscraper, for which the company provided building services, engineering, sustainability consulting and structural-engineering services, in collaboration with Lendlease,

came at the perfect time. They had long hoped for a new office that would be a safe, strong building that would stand the test of time, a place where staff could work comfortably and that would be innovative in its design. Though more and more countries are building timber skyscrapers these days, 25 King—one of the world's largest commercial timber office buildings to date, at 52 meters high—met all of Aurecon's requirements.

Above all, it was important that the building have a familiar quality, something uncharacteristic of an engineering company. "[We wanted] our staff to leave work feeling better than when they arrived [and] to feel like they were coming home when they came to work," says Aurecon's

Reception area on the first floor (the equivalent of the second floor in Japan). The space is as open and as relaxing as the offices. The placement of a concierge instead of a reception desk is another way to create a sense of familiarity.

Senior Project Engineer, Phillip Saal. Timber buildings are a way of upending the cold image of concrete office buildings. The redeveloped area, at a slight remove from the hustle and bustle of the city, also matches the building's mood. Even the ground level conveys Aurecon's intentions of creating a "home." Furniture is laid out loosely in the open space, and can be moved freely, depending on usage, to allow for smooth, casual communication.

There's another thing that is noticeably different from the previous office: according to Sarah McMahon, an Associate Principal at the architecture firm Woods Bagot (which undertook the fit-out of the Aurecon tenancy), there seems to be a current trend in Australia to move offices from higher floors to lower levels, and Aurecon intended to do the same.

"The developer, Lendlease, assumed that we'd want the top, because we are the anchor tenant of the building. And we said no, we want to engage [with the street]," says Aurecon's Senior Project Engineer, Nicholas Weiske.

"Being able to walk in from the street, straight into our fit-out—that's the experience we wanted," says Saal.

Soon, the employees did indeed begin to work that way. Since moving offices, more workers have started to use the stairs. After arriving in the morning, the staff head to the staircase in the center of the building and soak up the morning sun shining through the building's large windows as they climb up. Putting a large staircase in

1. The second-floor offices emphasize wooden surfaces. There are workstations that adapt to workers' needs, including normal, low, and elevated desks.
2. CLT (cross laminated timber) is used as the main building material. Components were provided by the developer Lendlease's own manufacturing business, illustrating their commitment to timber construction.
3. Booths for quiet and focused work. Meetings aren't allowed here, and the booths can't be reserved ahead of time, so they are first-come, first-served.
4. The communication hub, located in the center of the floor. Workers take a breather over coffee and sandwiches. The area can also be used for informal meetings.
5. "I love our entry stairs. Every day I come up the stairs," says Weiske.
6. An area known as the "Zen Room." Electronic devices such as PCs are not allowed. It's a space to get away from technology and feel refreshed. There are coloring books provided, access to greenery and natural light, and calming music playing, all of which are believed to be effective for relieving stress.
7. Aboriginal Australians value frank exchanges during meetings, and typically do not assign leaders. Taking a cue from such practices, these polygonal desks are meant to remove hierarchies.

the middle of a building comes with major risks—it would be a waste of a considerable investment if it wasn't used. "But people really embraced it," says Weiske. "People use them far more than the lift."

This isn't the only feature devised to create a sense of "home." The lampshades that illuminate the interior are made by Aboriginal Australian artists. Meeting rooms are named after native plants and indigenous words. Polygonal tables, which eschew seating hierarchies, are also inspired by indigenous ways of thinking. The same goes for ABW. "[Depending] on the task someone is undertaking, they might want to find some quiet space. They might need to meet with another person so they can collaborate. That's the beauty of a fit-out that is so flexible in nature," McMahon says. In addition to the versatility of the office space, importance is placed on creating a healthy work environment, allowing for adaptability through remote-work and flex hours. This is a surprising policy for an engineering company—it's no wonder that nearly 40% of Aurecon's employees are women.

On one occasion, 300 visitors were invited for a tour of the office, all of whom praised the space for not being like a typical engineering company. No one feels this more strongly than the workers here. "It's a much more casual space, so I think that encourages you to talk more," says Saal. Weiske continues, "I've worked here for twelve years, and the first day [in the new building] I sat down next to someone I hadn't met before. I said 'Hi, I'm Nick,' and right from day one everyone felt [...] that it was the right environment to meet people." WS

Nicholas Weiske
Senior Project Engineer
Aurecon

Phillip Saal
Senior Project Engineer
Aurecon

Sarah McMahon
Associate Principal
Woods Bagot

Aurecon's design philosophy

The seven key drivers for Aurecon's new office. The many terms relating to mindfulness reflect the modern workplace. When it comes to wellness, the building earned WELL Core and Shell certification at the Platinum level—it's believed to be the world's first timber building and Queensland's first building to achieve this honor.

Authenticity

Bravery

Connection

Wellness

Creation

Poetry

Passion

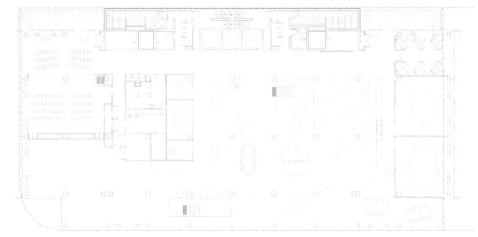

LEVEL 1

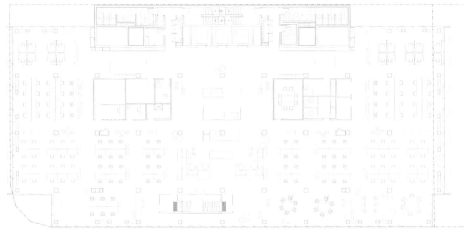

LEVEL 2

Office layout examples. The first floor (second floor in Japan) serves as the reception area and has meeting rooms. The second floor is a standard office space for workers.

Scale 1 : 500

1. The many plants that fill the space bring a sense of "home" and calm to the office.

2. Children's activity room. Australian law states that children under twelve should not be home alone. On days when children finish school early, they can play here. Children were in the offices when we visited as well.

3. Concierge on the first floor. Rather than a typical formal reception desk, the concierge aids visitors in a casual way. The lampshades are works by Aboriginal Australian artists.

4. In consideration of workers' health, the service counter stocks over twenty kinds of nuts/seeds/dried berries. These types of healthy snacks are gaining attention in Australia for their ability to regulate blood-sugar levels.

5. The ground-floor lobby, the building's common area, is accented with greenery. Another shared building amenity is the large bike storage area.

6. The office entrance. The street-facing café was opened to bring the liveliness of the street into the offices. The surrounding residences and offices were also designed to create ground-floor activity.

7. Building exterior: Ten floors with a total area of 15,000 square meters. The timber used in the building emits lower CO_2 emissions, and is sourced from sustainably managed forests.

Woodside

**The world's greatest smart building
supports workers using naturalistic technology**

*

Woodside
Perth
Established: 1954
Employees: 3,823 (2019)
Revenue: 343 million USD (2019)

In Perth, Western Australia's tourist destination, there is a smart building—the headquarters of the energy giant Woodside—that's been dubbed the greatest in the world. In honor of the Indigenous heritage of the area, the building is named Mia Yellagonga, meaning "place of Yellagonga," after the peoples' leader. Woodside's main business is locating oil and gas reserves; although they were ahead of their competition in the use of technology, they wanted to bring their technology into their workplaces as well, to enable speedy and efficient decisions and to help lead the company into the future.

"They needed to find the best benchmarks in the world," explains Simon Pole, the Global Design Director at Unispace, the firm responsible for the workplace's design. Visiting more than thirty of the newest buildings around the world, Woodside sought to find ways to bring amenities, sustainability, wellbeing, workspace, connectivity, technology, and innovation into one campus. "They wanted to make sure that this project was not only for 2018 but for 15 years beyond," says Pole. With a 15-year lease on the building, the concept for the office had to last just as long—Mia Yellagonga is meant to be an office from 15 years into the future.

One of the building's most noteworthy features is the "technology ecosystem" that manages the entire building. This system is derived from the company's business. Three years

These stairs connect all nineteen floors of Building A. By increasing the "bump factor," the stairs encourage chance encounters among workers, who tend to be divided on different floors, while its complex construction avoids monotony.

The family zone. Workers' families can use the space at any time. Children can come by and finish homework after school. It's an important feature in a country where laws prohibit children under twelve from staying home alone. There is also a restaurant serving healthy food.

before the project began, Woodside began to integrate AI to smartly and remotely operate its platforms and global refinery plants, as well as the ships and freight trains that travel between them. All the collected information was uploaded into IBM's Watson to derive optimal solutions to their logistical needs. Next, they developed Willow, a voice-interface program. Like Amazon's Alexa, the cognitive assistant answers when you speak to it. "Watson needed to understand about the oil and gas industry and understand the way [the business] worked," says Pole.

With this system as a foundation, various building-management systems, including middleware from Siemens, were connected and integrated into what they call the "technology ecosystem," making Mia Yellagonga one of the world's greatest smart buildings.

For example, Cisco's Spark system has been integrated for use in digital conferencing. Systems within the building can detect how many people are in a given area. What happens when you give Watson the data showing that five people are using a twelve-person-capacity meeting room? Next time, the system will direct people to a smaller meeting room, and the larger room will go to a different team.

But Mia Yellagonga doesn't flaunt its technology. Instead, the technology is intended to be natural and invisible. Contactless biometric authentication (face, fingerprints, and vein scanning) is used for entering the building, allowing people to pass through smoothly without stopping. Sensors and a dedicated app also allow for tracking the real-time location of workers. "They wanted the technology to [aid] in the decision-making and the processing, but they didn't want it everywhere and visible. They wanted to make a very friendly building on the inside. To do that, we focused on the wellbeing and the synergies of the life and work aspects," explains Pole.

For instance, by connecting the nineteen floors with stairs, the designers encouraged the "bump factor" by creating chance encounters between workers moving between floors. Workspaces are made as flexible as possible, to allow employees to freely choose where they want to work. Unispace defines workspaces in four modes: "focus work," meaning individuals working alone; "collaboration work," for work in groups; "learning mode," meaning activities with an emphasis on learning; and "socializing mode," meaning interactions amongst workers. These modes cannot be contained in one workspace. Rather than implementing ABW or open floor plans, Woodside offers over 60 different work settings, reflecting a workspace philosophy they call "Rightspace." In addition, the colors and materials used in the interiors reflect the six seasons within Aboriginal culture. After all, Woodside employs a diverse group of workers. There are older generations of engineers as well as young data scientists fresh out of college. "We had to make sure the workspace was flexible enough for now to accommodate the generations, but also into the future," says Pole. WS

1. Executives' floor. The executives, who previously worked in closed offices, wanted to "share information quicker," so private rooms were replaced by more open spaces.
2. Advanced Operations. A space for external partners to come and go. Groups can study 3D designs shared in real time using AI and VR.
3. A VIP room for entertaining clients. There is also a restaurant that can prepare full-course meals.
4. Technology hub. A one-stop shop for IT-equipment repair and replacement for workers on the move with laptops and smartphones.
5. A café on the lower floor, available to workers and their families. It's open 24 hours a day, 365 days a year, providing a relaxed work atmosphere.
6. Learning and wellness floor. There are rooms for training, a library, and a napping area. It's also a "Wi-fi Not-spot," a place to take a break from technology and digitally detox.

Four-way floor design

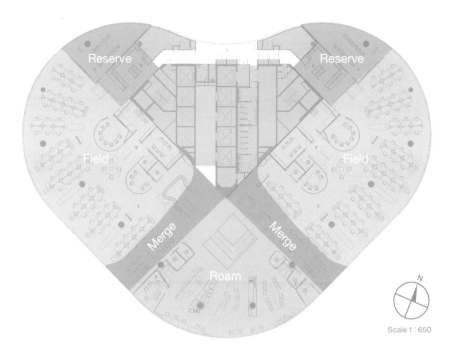

Scale 1 : 650

Building A's 10th through 27th floors have a standard layout, with four types of spaces. The central area connected to the stairs is the "Roam" area, for informal and collaborative work. "Reserve" areas are project rooms. "Merge" areas are collaboration booths. "Field" areas (pictured) are spaces for focused work.

Dramatic increase in worker satisfaction

Rightspace	Utilization	Collaboration	Connectivity	Focus
0% → **92**%	39% → **78**%	40% → **65**%	30% → **92**%	60% → **60**%

Pride	Wellbeing	Moral	Creative Thinking	Productivity
62% → **92**%	42% → **82**%	64% → **82**%	35% → **85**%	**200**% up

The results of a post-occupancy evaluation, administered to workers nine months after relocating to Mia Yellalonga. Improvements can be seen in many areas, including communication, collaboration, motivation, and productivity.*
*Based on the work process engineering measured, time was halved.

7. Mia Yellagonga is made up of four buildings, A through D. The 32 floors can accommodate up to 5,000 workers; about 3,200 people currently work there. The site includes an innovation center, a retail market, an atrium, a child-care center, and a wellness center.
8. Building B (pictured) contains facilities that support workers' training and health, such as a gym and training facilities. Building C is a facility for collaborations with universities and other external organizations. Building D contains a robotics lab designed with NASA and MIT.

Arup

"Living Arup"—
A user focused vision

Arup
Melbourne
Established: 1946
Employees: Approximately 15,500 (2019)
Revenue: 1.71 billion GBP (2019)
(Data applies to the company worldwide)

Arup, an engineering, planning, and design company, headquartered in London, offers new ways of working not typical of engineering companies. The physical structure is unique, with two mezzanines connecting three floors, but their company culture is even more particular. "A unique aspect of Arup is our ownership structure, where the company is held in trust for the benefit of all members," Arup's Workplace Leader, Cameron McIntosh, points out.

As an employee-owned organization, Arup has the freedom to select the projects that it undertakes, without the need to consider outside shareholders.

Implementing Activity Based Working (ABW), an approach atypical of an engineering company, was also proposed by the staff themselves. In 2015, a set of Australasian regional workplace guidelines were developed by Hassell in partnership with Arup, incorporating the drivers and philosophy of the firm. The detailed interpretation and implementation of those guidelines is unique to each local office. In Melbourne, they arrived at a workplace vision dubbed "Living Arup," which focuses on sustainability, wellness, connectivity, and flexibility.

Their new office embodies this concept of "Living Arup," which in turn also plays a role in supporting a flexible work culture: one team and collaboration driven by connectivity across the space. Managers participated in all design meetings

Three floors are loosely connected by mezzanines. Wire mesh is used instead of glass partitions, a lower-maintenance option that allows for improved visual connectivity.

for the new space, and all project decisions were reached after their discussions.

Rather than separating the three individual floors, the mezzanines connect them to create a space that is a "three-dimensional volume." Each floor is visually connected, despite the office's vast 2,000-square-meter floor area. "On a personal level, it might be inconvenient for me to walk from level three to level one to get a coffee, but on a business level and a wellbeing point, that works," says McIntosh. The work desks are divided into neighborhoods that serve as each group's address, but the groups move once every four months. Staff can move freely around the office with their laptops, but lunch is usually in the kitchen. "This space is our home space," says McIntosh. "We've got a number of microwaves, stoves, [and] fridges. We encourage people away from their desk at lunch, and […] then they tend to sit down and have a chat with someone. Whilst we don't have a rule that says don't eat at your desk, it's about encouraging people to come together. Even if we're having an event [in the café] upstairs, our staff still has somewhere to go."

For sustainability, the company uses electrolyzed water instead of chemicals for cleaning. There is a unisex changing room, complete with showers for staff who commute by

1. Work lounge/café space near the entrance. The space is operated by the social enterprise STREAT, which works to provide disadvantaged youth with training and work experience.
2. An elevated Sky Park sits 11m above the ground directly in front of the office, offering a place for staff to take breaks during the day. The area will be expanded once development is completed.
3. Building exterior. The area, Melbourne Quarter, is a redeveloped precinct with office buildings, residences, and commercial establishments. One Melbourne Quarter houses Arup's offices.

bicycle. There are also yoga, pilates, and personal-training spaces, which allow staff to exercise whenever they want.

What is Arup's approach to technology? "Technology is a tool, not an outcome in itself. Even in reception, we wanted that experience to be a very human experience, so there are no big screens or digital waterfalls, because that wasn't what we wanted the experience to be," says McIntosh. "To allow a seamless experience, the same access card is used for building access down to locker access. The electronic locks on the lockers also mean we don't have to manage sets of keys for the next eleven years. [...] And we can monitor that data [to] see if someone hasn't accessed their locker for six months, and [...] we can ask them, 'Do you need your locker?' We can assign a visitor a locker for a week. All the technology decisions were about improving the operation."

All of the above decisions were made with the employee outcome in mind. "For many things, as a percentage of the budget, it wasn't much at all. But it's the bits staff interact with every day that make a big difference to their experience," McIntosh says confidently. Thanks to these efforts, Arup's reputation continues to grow. In an employee survey taken three months after the move, 98% reported that they were satisfied. The fact that the office has grown from 453 staff members to 520 in the year since moving proves the success of the new space. In addition to a number of design awards, the new Arup Melbourne Workplace has achieved a 6 Star Green Star Rating and Platinum WELL Certification under WELL v2—one of the first workplaces in Australia and globally to earn the distinction. WS

1. Kitchen space. Employees bring their own meals, but fruit and salad are provided. "We're looking into potentially providing breakfast and [...] cooking demonstrations," says McIntosh.
2. Office space on the top floor. Neighborhoods are roughly assigned to each team, while still incorporating ABW. Teams move every four months to prevent communication from becoming static.
3. Meetings can be held in the Garden Lounge while enjoying natural light and air. Over 600 plants fill the office, supporting wellbeing both visually and through increased oxygen. Indoor air quality is also constantly monitored for pollutants.
4. Reception. This is a welcoming space, more akin to a hospitality setting, with staff there to immediately greet you. Beyond the reception is the work lounge and café by STREAT.

5. 500 lockers in a single location. There is also a support center, where staff members can consult with one another on their way to storing their belongings.

6. Since many staff members commute by bicycle, the facility is equipped with changing rooms, showers, and more than 80 bicycle-storage spaces. In Australia, facilities like these are called "end-of-trip facilities."

7. Another major objective for the new office was to allow for facilities geared toward experimentation and innovation. This is a light lab, for testing various lighting fixtures.

8. A sound lab, for testing the acoustics of spaces before they are built. Here, the effects can be actually experienced before finalizing the design.

9. A fabrication lab, equipped with laser cutters and 3D printers. Staff make use of the space, but it's also used in engineering programs for high-school students.

10. All floors and teams are visually connected. The open visual sightlines and stairs promote chance interaction and help facilitate better communication. "Staff can see each other and meet, rather than call or email," says McIntosh.

11. The ground-floor kitchen, as seen from the top floor. In addition to the plentiful natural light, the office is equipped with lighting systems that reproduce circadian rhythms, with the aim of improving wellness.

Cameron McIntosh
Workplace Leader
Arup

FOCUS 1

Designing experiences
rooted in culture

James Calder

ERA-co
Global Director
User Strategy
James Calder

Joined the architectural firm Woods Bagot after
graduating from university. Founded Calder
Consultants in 2012, where he has worked on a
number of workplace designs and change
management, primarily in Australia. In November
2019, the company relaunched as the experience
consultancy Agency ERA-co.

Organizations have become more flexible, with the ability to adjust where and when people work—it's easy to work remotely through Zoom and Skype, and old business models that only utilize limited technology are being phased out. James Calder, a workplace futurist who has specialized in consulting on workplaces in Australia and globally through Calder Consultants, sees that "It's the same [in Australia] as lots of places."

In the lexicon of spatial planning, this manifests as "diversity"—not a completely closed office or a completely open plan, but a hybrid of the two.

"Some organizations won't let anyone own a desk, but others are saying you should own a desk, it's okay to not have to ABW. We're seeing a real mixture. I think that hybrids are good for most organizations," says Calder.

The emphasis on user experience is also evident. The day is near, if not yet realized, when you will be able to control connections to systems for space reservations, food and drink, and locker use. But, as Calder points out, "before user experience is the organizational culture and the values."

People prefer to group with others that have similar personalities and goals. For a person who is part of an older culture, traditional offices are hard to escape. Conversely, for some tech companies, working in everyday clothes in an office with beer and food is also "actually part of their culture." They wear T-shirts because they like T-shirts. The offices have beer and food because workers who work longer hours don't want to waste time shopping. The way people work is an expression of culture.

All this means that it's difficult for external people, like building owners, to provide these types of user experiences.

"I think organizations need to manage that very carefully themselves—the people that were in People and Culture or Facility Management or Technology now need to come together and have a focus on the culture of the organization," says Calder.

Last year, Calder relaunched Calder Consultants as ERA-co and updated their consulting solutions. Under the sponsorship of the architectural-design firm Woods Bagot, anthropologists, business analysts, and data scientists were gathered to tackle not only workplace consulting but also larger corporate issues, such as branding. What will Calder's future offices look like?

"I don't think we're going to build just plain office buildings anymore," says Calder. "I think the amount of normal office space is reducing, and the amount of shared space, meeting space, food, beverage, lifestyle, work style is increasing. And, also, what's changing is that the tenant's businesses are so dynamic, they can't take long-term leases anymore. [It's impossible to] commit to ten years with any certainty about how much space they need. So a lot of the leases

1. 80 Collins Street, currently under construction in Melbourne. Calder developed the concept for this complex. Located in Melbourne's business and commercial center, it consists of two office towers and low-rise commercial area.
2. ERA-co, a new consultancy launched with Woods Bagot. Going beyond office design, they help develop experience-based solutions for companies. The consultancy holds offices in New York, Melbourne, Sydney, London, and Shanghai.

we are now doing are now kind of flexi-leases, [which say] this is the core space that we want, this is the flex space that we want, this is the shared space that we want you as the building owner to provide."

These technologies now enable people to "connect" remotely; the emergence of a younger generation that enjoys this kind of "connection" will continue to change offices. "[Buildings] are moving away from tenancies of leased space to become business communities. We are now actually creating networks within buildings that create ecosystems for different clusters of industry types," says Calder. Moving between digital and physical formats will also become more seamless. Culture influences physical and digital experiences.

"That's why we've invested with software developers and data scientists and people that can start to link up the Internet of Things (IoT) within buildings. And we're starting to talk with the service companies," says Calder. "To take that to its logical conclusion, I think we're nearly at a point where all the systems in a building will actually be managed remotely, in the cloud,

and we'll have much better data sets about how to manage efficiency, sustainability, but the experience as well. Instead of just looking at individual buildings, we'll have whole global data sets of users. I think we'll end up with a much better-integrated user experience, physical and virtual, and also we'll end up with buildings where the systems are run a lot more productively, a bit like a jet. The engines are not run by the airlines, they are run by either GE or Rolls Royce and they manage them in the cloud. [...] I think that's what will happen in buildings."

What does it mean for buildings to become cloud-based?

"Organizations will aggregate things like lighting, air-conditioning, information, lifts," says Calder. "Things like lifts will be owned by the lift companies, and the owner of the building will just pay as they go. I think a lot of the systems at the moment are measuring the wrong things—the devices that can do things, but we haven't worked out yet what we want them to do. We can measure utilization, but it doesn't tell us anything about the quality of what people are doing. There are some good apps that are

being developed. Some of them are coming from a social-networking point of view. They tend to work much better, but they're actually not connected to the building yet. We're still at a stage where we've got to merge a number of directions into one unified system—I think we're probably five to ten years away from that. It's a difficult area because the people that control the buildings, the big real-estate companies that control facility management, they're not natural innovators. They're much more conservative organizations. I think we don't seem to have a very good system as an industry to innovate."

This points to one of the main things that Calder wants to accomplish through ERA-co. Technology companies are unfamiliar with new ways of working and issues in the office, whereas tenants and clients are interested in these things but are less technology-focused.

"For the first time, I've seen, just in the last year or so, large global workplace teams for big companies start to bring technology people into their property group," says Calder. "I think that's the beginning of starting to solve those issues." **WS**

RMIT University

**An urban campus
open to the people of the city**

★

RMIT University
Melbourne
Founded: 1887
Student population: 86,839 (2018)

The main campus of RMIT University is located in central Melbourne. It could be called an urban campus, but the campus was previously closed off, with its back to the street, despite occupying prime city real estate. Isolated from the vibrancy of the surrounding area, the campus continued to accumulate unthoughtful additions to its structure that didn't contribute to the metro area. "We had to open up our campus and change the campus dynamic," says Nicole Eaton, of Campus Planning and Services at RMIT.

The campus-renewal project, called New Academic Street/NAS, aimed to open the closed-off campus to the city. The solution was simple. Gates were opened up to allow people to come and go, and retail and public spaces were created through the development of new laneways that run through the campus's grounds and facilities. Students and citizens can sit next to one another on benches, indistinguishable. Newly developed public spaces are open to all, bringing to campus the bustle of the city at all hours of the day.

The campus's relationship to the street wasn't the only important shift. The interiors were also changed significantly, making the campus a much more comfortable place for students. "It was the notion of introducing a sticky campus," explains Eaton.

In the past, RMIT students had no choice but to leave campus as soon

The center of the campus, on Bowen Street. Nothing separates the campus from the street, and both students and passersby come and go. The outdoor furniture is placed freely around the area.

1. The new arcade that runs through the main campus connects two streets, allowing both students and citizens to pass through freely. It is emblematic of a campus opened up to the city.
2. Outdoor communication space, also open to the public. Students are seen studying alongside business people holding meetings and citizens taking walks.
3. The ground-floor outdoor food court of the campus's environmentally friendly "Garden Building." There is a café operated by STREAT, which supports disadvantaged youth. NMBW Architecture Studio is responsible for the design.

as their classes ended. Australian universities don't have the same seminar (known as "zemi") and lab structures as Japanese universities, leaving students without a place to go after class. "There's nowhere for a student to come and put their bag and then go to buy some lunch or have class and come back," explains Marika Neustupny, a director at NMBW Architecture Studio, who were one of the architects for the new campus. As a result, many students would go to off-campus food courts or malls, skipping their afternoon classes. The challenge for the NAS project was to create an environment in which students could spend their entire day.

"[We've provided] these kinds of spaces where students can sit

on their own [to] study, or do some group activity. Students want to be on campus now. Particularly, you notice it with the students that live in the city, because they're living in student accommodation that is very small, [with only] a bed and a desk and a bathroom. But they come onto campus, and this is their living room. They're here until ten o'clock at night," says Eaton.

The architects who handled the design are Carey Lyon, a professor at RMIT, and four of his former students. Nigel Bertram, a director at NMBW Architecture Studio, is one of them. The previous campus was designed by a single architect, and the buildings were monolithic and regular. This time, however, five architects designed the twelve new

Nicole Eaton
Campus Planning and Services
RMIT University

Nigel Bertram
Director
NMBW Architecture Studio

Marika Neustupny
Director
NMBW Architecture Studio

buildings separately, while following a collaborative master plan drawn up by Lyon's architecture firm, Lyons. Together, the buildings look "more like the city within this block." For security, there are few hidden areas, with the high visibility allowing you to see from one building to the other. One major achievement on the technology side of things was the development of a campus-navigation app. Although still in its prototype phase, the app will provide students with all they need, including the ability to call security at the touch of a button, information on off-campus bus services, and the ability to reserve study rooms and materials.

Today, students can be seen on campus throughout the day. "I walk through here at five on a Friday and I wonder, What are all these students doing here? They're not necessarily doing work or studying, but they're using the campus," says Eaton. "We've got Melbourne University students coming here because it's so great." Just as planned, RMIT has successfully created a sticky campus.

There are more plans ahead. The Melbourne Innovation District is a concept in development that will link RMIT and Melbourne University, making the entire area a base for innovation. Although it's still in its planning stages, the Innovation District will create an even stronger impression that the university has changed. RMIT, which once literally turned its back to the city, is on the verge of becoming an influential presence in Melbourne. **WS**

A campus that opens toward the streets

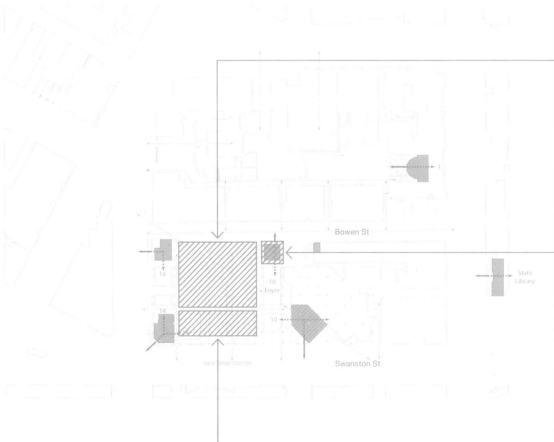

The Garden Building. Considering human scale, each building has been kept low, and all rooftops slope to connect to one another, allowing for seamless movement between buildings.

The campus is open toward the street. A subway station will be built on Swanston Street—there is currently a tram running there—and it is expected that the number of people using the campus will increase dramatically in the future.

By creating multiple laneways through a previously obstructive structure, the vibrancy of the city is invited into the campus.

1. An area for students to work on projects. Designed by five different architectural firms, each area has a completely different style of design. The variety of spaces stimulates learning.
2. Work lounge. This space is used for individual work and group projects. Relaxing rocking chairs are also in the space.
3. RMIT Connect is a one-stop shop for a variety of student services. A robust system provides quick and efficient support to busy students, many of whom commute to the urban campus.
4. Café. In an effort to increase public space, tenants only rent kitchen spaces. The tables and seating are free for anyone to use without purchasing a drink.
5. Campus corridor. Alongside the food stands, there are co-working desks for light work and meetings. Such places create a "sticky" effect.

Visible changes in the student body

10,000+
STUDENTS

Over 10,000 students participate in the NAS program

80+
BUSINESSES

Over 80 businesses by students and graduates in the pop-up space

54
EVENTS

54 events organized by students

Results of a survey of students since the campus renewal. These figures suggest that students have become more active and interested in the university.

Quay Quarter Tower

A vertical village creates a new community on Australia's doorstep

Photo: AMP Capital

Quay Quarter Tower
Sydney
Developer: AMP Capital
Completion: 2022
Total floor area: 102,000m²

Circular Quay, on Sydney Harbour, was the site where the first European settlers arrived in Australia. The area is dotted with numerous cultural and artistic institutions, including the Sydney Opera House, art galleries, and museums, and is also historically a financial district. It's an area of historical and cultural significance for Sydney. However, as Michael Wheatley, AMP Capital's Development Director, Quay Quarter, explains, "Nothing has happened in Circular Quay for decades, for a long time. The area has gotten a bit run down."

The ongoing development project aims to rejuvenate Circular Quay as a vibrant city while retaining its key qualities. AMP Capital, which has owned the land for more than sixty years, is the developer. Their first action was getting a development permit from the city of Sydney, which stipulated that the new work would not overshadow or have adverse impacts on the surrounding historic buildings.

"We worked with the council and [...] we agreed on a strategy to [retain and use the core 68% of the original structure built in 1970, making sure there is] no impact on the surrounding areas," says Wheatley.

The building is named Quay Quarter Tower. As you can see from the exterior, the concept of the building is a "Vertical Village," with five volumes stacked on top of one another. The aim is to create a sense of community, like a village, throughout the building. The five volumes are connected by an atrium and staircases to enhance

1. Quay Quarter Tower exterior. The five volumes of the building stack at angles to provide tenants with a view and a terrace without creating an overpowering presence in the surrounding area.

2. Office floor. Each of the five volumes of the building has a large atrium and spiral staircase to increase visibility between floors and encourage communication. Deloitte and AMP are scheduled to move in, and there are limited leasing opportunities for other companies.
3. Lower-level retail entrance. Quay Quarter Tower is looking for tenants that appeal to younger generations that value a mix of work and leisure, such as wellbeing retailers and restaurants with an emphasis on lifestyle and wellness.

communication and a sense of unity amongst the tenant companies. The five volumes are layered in a twisting fashion, creating shifting views for the higher-level floors and garden spaces at the top of each of the volumes and avoiding an overpowering impression on the lower levels and surrounding community. In order to provide enough public space for citizens to enjoy, alleyways and promenades connect the east, west, north, and south of the building, encouraging people to come and go. The project is expected to be completed in 2022. This attention toward tenants and the community has been well received by the market, with 75% of the total area already spoken for by future tenants, including AMP's headquarters and Deloitte's

Michael Wheatley
Development Director,
Quay Quarter
AMP Capital

Brian Donnelly
Senior Development Manager
Quay Quarter Tower

1. A view of the Circular Quay skyline, where Quay Quarter Tower will be located. The area is thriving as a long-standing center of cultural institutions within Sydney, and as a financial CBD. The Opera House can be seen on the wharf.
2. Terraces are located at the base of each "vertical village." The presence of these common areas fosters chance encounters and a sense of community. This is also a benefit of the twisted five-volume construction.
3. Quay Quarter Tower features a garden with public access, public art, and views.

Australian headquarters.

What about the movement toward intensifying technology usage? "People prefer to use existing apps [and] to use what they are already using," says Wheatley. He continues, "We have a term in English: You don't want to create a white elephant. A white elephant is this big thing that becomes redundant or useless down the track. You want it to be flexible and already part of their normal day. That way it's more seamless." Although this is a cutting-edge building, the developer's attitude toward technology is cautious. "The technology that we are talking about today [...] is going to be different from what it is in two years. As we get closer to the experiences that we want to curate [...] we'll then work out what the best technology is at the time, with the aim of being as flexible as possible to be continued to be upgraded. The operating pace of creating a building is completely different to the pace at which technology changes. This is why no one's ever really been able to bring it together successfully," Wheatley explains.

The company takes environmental considerations seriously as well. They received the highest rating, six, for their building design from Green Star, which evaluates companies' environmental impact. Meanwhile, their building-operation rating is slightly lower, at 5.5, but they don't seem to be deterred—their main focus is on people. "If you have a herb garden you'd get points [with Green Star], but [...] it doesn't really bring people together and create social community," says Wheatley.

Quay Quarter Tower's Senior Development Manager, Brian Donnelly, continues. "We've got a more genuine approach to health and wellness by making investments in the stairs, in the atriums, spaces that people, at the end of the day, want to use. It's better for you as a person because you'll get a bit of a workout on the stairs. It has that more social dynamic as well, because you might pass someone on the stairs. It assists in that informal information transfer, which is critical to organizations as well. But we don't get any points for [such humanistic approaches] with the rating tools." **WS**

4. The Lifestyle area, or shopping mall. There are plans for activations and a variety of events.
5. On the right hand side of the image is Quay Quarter Tower. The area is lined with apartments, stylish bars and restaurants, lifestyle and wellbeing retail, and a variety of other entertainment that will transform the old, bleak financial district into a beautiful new neighborhood.

Convenient street access

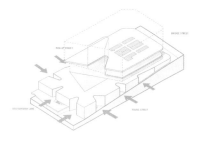

The lower level, called the podium, has a lush garden, restaurants, and retail stores. The multiple street-facing entrances visually connect to the central atrium space and promote pedestrian flow.

Beautiful views in all directions

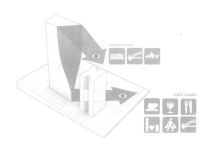

By stacking each of the five volumes at slight angles, the lower floors open up toward the community and the higher floors provide residents with views and rooftop gardens without overpowering the surrounding area. This isn't just good design—it also provides rational solutions to practical problems.

Retaining the old structure in the new design

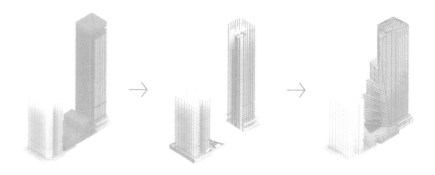

Quay Quarter Tower upcycles the existing core of the old building, which was built in 1970. The unique construction method of making additions while retaining 68% of the structure is a sustainable solution that shortens construction time. Four new elevator shafts will be added to the core, and approximately 45,000m² of new additions will be added to the north side.

CASE 8

Mirvac

An experiential showcase of one company's innovations

Mirvac
Sydney
Established: 1972
Employees: 1,540 (2019)

For the innovative real-estate developer Mirvac, the firm responsible for projects like South Eveleigh (Page 84), its own office, named the EY Centre at Sydney, was a chance to showcase their innovations as an experience for customers. Flexibility is one of the key concepts behind the 7,000m² office space, which spans six floors of the building. A variety of features, including fixed desks, high benches, and collaboration spaces, allow workers to choose their space according to what work style is needed that day. Agile working solutions, including working from home, is also encouraged. According to Simon Healy, the General Manager of Commercial Development at Mirvac, "If you're productive and your manager is comfortable with how you're performing, then you can work outside of the office."

Workplace dynamic density, which takes into consideration how many people are assigned to one workstation, is also a key innovation in Mirvac's offices. As more employees travel for meetings or take advantage of agile working policies, it's unnecessary to assign individual workstations to each employee. Workplace dynamic density tends to grow along with the size of companies. "Typically, Mirvac's running with a dynamic density of 20% here, which means that we [have] 12 people who can comfortably occupy ten workstations," says Healy. In the building as a whole, the space is designed with a density of eight

A café operated by YWCA NSW, a women's-support charity organization. The space's rent is waived, and the profits from the café go towards funding the YWCA NSW's support services for women experiencing domestic violence.

square meters of space per work point (10 to 12 square meters per work point is standard in Australia for newly built offices). Furthermore, the population density shifts fluidly because of agile work (the term for ABW typically used in Australia). According to Mirvac's data on employee satisfaction, productivity has gone up 35%, and the approval of the visual aesthetics of the office have gone from 30 to 91%. Workers' acknowledgment of the "positive health impact of the workplace" has also increased, from 33 to 88%.

Six architectural firms were commissioned to create concept designs for the building. "[Office buildings] are typically designed in a rectangular shape. They're glass, they're concrete, they're shiny, but they don't have much character. Yes, it has to be an office building and capable of housing commercial tenants, but we wanted the EY Centre to look and feel a bit different," said Healy. Through the design-competition process, Sydney architectural firm FJMT's design was chosen. Mirvac was satisfied with the curved design that also utilized wood; the triple-glazed façade system was particularly ambitious. The external system uses three layers of glass to provide shade from the sun, with wooden venetian blinds installed in the enclosed space between the three layers to allow the warmth of the wood to be displayed in both the interior and the exterior of the building.

1. EY Centre, which stands at 200 George Street in Sydney. Mirvac developed the building, and their office occupies the 26th through 31st floors. It's characterized by its curvilinear forms and wooden textures.
2. The design implements a triple-glazed façade system, which uses three layers of glass. These wooden blinds add a gentle atmosphere to the building. As you get closer, the variations in wood grain become clear.

Simon Healy
General Manager
Commercial Development
Mirvac

What does Mirvac predict for the future of the office market? One trend they're forecasting is the return to the office. While environments enabling people to "work anywhere" have been developed, the value of working in an office has become apparent. Many companies have realized that offices where people gather are good places to foster collaboration and culture.

"The office is really important for a firm's culture and for an employee's sense of belonging. There has been a lot of talk recently that 'everyone is going to continue to work remotely.' In fact, many companies are now realizing that, actually, people like to go to work, people like to collaborate, and people like to have that human connection," said Healy.

Public and retail space in office buildings are on the rise for the same reasons. Also, many Australian companies seek to honor the country's traditions and Indigenous cultures through design and artwork. "That's the humanistic side of buildings. Everyone loves a nice piece of public art, everyone likes to go and see some remnants of history or the way that you might creatively interpret the history of the site. We certainly do that on all our developments. When we talk to office tenants, they're saying that as well. What's the retail like, what's the public art, what's the cultural significance of this building? Does this building have a soul? Does it feel good when I come in? That's becoming increasingly important," says Healy. WS

1. The building's ground-floor common entrance, furnished with comfortable, relaxing furniture and a wall mural that pays homage to Indigenous people. The aim was to create a hotel-like atmosphere rather than an office.
2. At the end of each flight of stairs is a communication hub. A training center and a kitchen also help to encourage chance encounters between employees.
3. Agile working allows employees the freedom to choose when and where they want to work. Enclosed concentration booths are popular.
4. A long kitchen is located along a main thoroughfare in the office. The sheer volume of traffic triggers chance encounters. It's also a landing pad that doubles as a work space.
5. The six floors that Mirvac occupies have an internal staircase in the center to stimulate employee interaction. Facial-recognition security systems have been adopted to allow employees to move about smoothly.

FOCUS 2

Changing the future of workplaces through super-experiences

Super-Experience

Paul Edwards
General Manager
Workplace Experiences
Mirvac

Paul works to create exceptional experiences at Mirvac's commercial buildings and to define and shape the future of work. He has recently researched "super-experiences", in collaboration with Worktech Academy, which is led by Jeremy Myerson an expert in workplace research. In February 2019, he published the paper "The Super-Experience: Designing for Talent in the Digital Workplace."

In today's global digital economy, it's a given that companies must provide great work experiences, attract and retain top talent, and drive innovation and creativity. That's why Mirvac emphasizes the importance of "super-experiences" in the workplaces they provide. The quickest way to understand this concept is to learn about how retail has changed.

Since the birth of Amazon over 15 years ago, retail businesses have been asking, "Why do we have shopping centers?" The answer lies in the fact that "people like to shop because it's an experience, which is something Amazon can't replicate or replace." As such, businesses have been trying to connect retail with experiences. Food courts became dining centers; bowling alleys and movie theaters were added as an extension to shopping centers. Paul Edwards, General Manager of Workplace Experiences at Mirvac, said, "Instead of just going for a burger, you'd now go and have a nice lunch with some champagne and then go shopping for some shoes." That's what bringing together experience and retail is all about.

With that mindset, how do we connect experiences and workplaces? "In Australia, Baby Boomers will be replaced in droves by the digitally minded Millennial generation by 2024. With the rapid advances in technology, there's no doubt that it is going to change the workplace forever. Employees need to [continuously] learn new skills to keep up. How do we help people to continuously learn and how do we create new learning experiences?" said Edwards.

Mirvac has begun researching not only everyday experiences but also super-experiences, a term that refers to transcendent experiences that affect creativity and emotion.

"Our definition of what constitutes a super-experience is something awe-inspiring, and dramatic, something that makes you stand up and go, 'Wow, that's amazing,'" says Edwards. This sort of inspiration can lead employees to think and be creative in new ways.

"There are three key factors which make up a super-experience: awe-inspiring, curated, and learning. As we move away from logical, standard experiences towards empathy and creativity [...] this will help generate a new interest for people around work," says Edwards.

How do you create a super-experience? What is a client's goal or problem to be solved? What experiences make people want to be in an office, and, conversely, what experiences inhibit them from feeling that way? For example, Edwards describes how Mirvac improved the entry experience for customers when visiting their head office at the EY Centre in Sydney. "When customers arrived at our reception desk, there was often a queue and it would take a long time to register each person's details to gain access into the building. We wanted to simplify this process for our visitors, so we examined the steps that each person takes when they arrive and identified the problems. As a result, we developed a new system that sends an email with entry instructions to each visitor before they arrive. This has allowed them to gain faster access into the building, reducing the time significantly and improving the experience for our guests," said Edwards.

"In the future, I'd like to think that as soon as a guest is within 100 meters of our building, it sends me a text [...], the gates open for the visitor and they know what lift they're going to. However, we can't just think of this process as only using technology, as the human element is also very important. We would also still have a concierge to greet visitors and make them feel welcome," says Edwards.

Not only is Mirvac implementing super-experiences at their head office, they are also developing new ways to bring experiences to their portfolio of commercial buildings throughout Australia. Some of these initiatives include creating an urban farm in underutilized spaces, and installing interactive artwork in the lobbies. **WS**

How super-experiences are born

Clarity — Empathy

Wellbeing

Efficiency — Innovation

Super-Experience

Learning

Optimization — Intrigue

Diagram of the super-experience. As an experience moves from the realm of clarity and optimization into the realm of complexity and empathy, a super-experience emerges.

Hoist, a flexible office entirely owned by Mirvac.

Part of the office parking garage at Mirvac's EY Centre building was converted into a farm to add value back into underutilized space. A group of employees tend to the farm, with 94% of the group feeling happier and less stressed as a result.

How can we prevent technology from getting the best of us?
Australian practices for avoiding a "degradation of emotions"

Editor-in-Chief: Shotaro Yamashita

**When ABW—a decentralized way of working—and technology converge,
it is easy to envision a future in which individuals become subservient to technology.
How is Australia fighting against this?**

Humans "mobilized" by technology

Technology is an integral part of our lives. I live my daily life in an environment where I can open my smartphone and be presented with information that is optimized for me, where everything, including shopping, is within reach. If we follow the "pace layering" framework for social change presented by the writer and editor Stewart Brand, the first major shifts will occur in areas closest to consumers, like fashion

and commerce. Today, the use of personal data-based technologies developed for consumers is creeping into the traditional white-collar workplace. As Alex Rosenblat points out in "Uberland: How Algorithms Are Rewriting the Rules of Work," algorithms are already manipulating and playing with workers in the short-term labor market, also known as the gig economy. The book illustrates that, although the cost of managing drivers is extremely low and the compensation paid to drivers and the flexibility of labor are

achieved at a high level, drivers are losing ambition, and Uber, which provides the algorithms, does not recognize them as workers, acting only as a provider of software that matches users and self-employed workers and thus abandoning its social responsibility to protect them.

Why does technology that is meant to help people alienate them? The philosopher Martin Heidegger called the characteristics of modern technology since the industrial revolution "Gestell"; he described such technology as functioning

solely for the purpose of using natural energy efficiently, beyond the intentions of the humans who created it. The current situation in the gig economy suggests that people are being utilized as another kind of "renewable energy," mobilized by technology solely in terms of their usefulness.

Decentralization leads to a "degradation of emotions"

In a world where workers are dominated directly by algorithms,

Shotaro Yamashita

Director of the Workstyle Lab. at Kokuyo Co., Ltd.
Researcher and consultant on the future of the
workplace. Visiting research fellow at the Helen
Hamlyn Centre for Design at the Royal College of
Arts in England, 2016-2017.

as in the case of Uber, things are determined by correlation rather than by any humanly imaginable causation, and dull labor, in which it's impossible to make sense of these directives, pervades. Workers lose their humanity and become driven instead only by profit and loss. The sociologist Shinji Miyadai calls this behavior, in which individuals become enslaved to the system, the "degradation of emotions."

In the past, companies functioned as a "community" that their employees could rely on, and they were willing to work for the good of society, their departments, and their colleagues. In Japan, following its period of rapid economic growth, companies have replaced local communities as workers migrate en masse from rural areas to urban centers. However, maintaining community norms became difficult as organizations expanded, and the sense of community faded further as companies began to create competition among workers through meritocracy and to use expendable labor, such as temp workers. In addition, technology has made decentralized labor (ABW) a reality, thereby accelerating the dilution of the organization.

On the other hand, a way of working without time and place constraints, like ABW, can be very effective in increasing flexibility, which is a matter of utmost importance in developed countries with declining working populations.

However, with the movement of highly individualized workers becoming the norm, human management through supervisors becomes difficult; in its place, a trend toward tracking workers with data such as location and work information has become prominent. By getting rid of the

middleman that once supported a sense of community through departments or co-workers that share the same office, workers are managed directly by the company through smartphones and laptops, an emerging system that is prone to create a degradation of emotions. At present, one-on-one and group meetings spearheaded by middle management barely manages to foster a sense of community by connecting members.

Already, decentralized societies (emblemized by practices like ABW) are weakening communities and causing loneliness, creating a global social issue. The U.K. made loneliness the biggest health issue of our time: the country established a Minister for Loneliness in 2018, the first position of its kind in the world. Another view is that the combination of discretionary labor and performance-based work creates a situation in which employees are encouraged to work longer hours to compensate for being evaluated only in terms of numbers. ABW that goes too far leads to a hollowing out of the community and individual exhaustion.

When considering the governance of companies that have expanded globally, the use of technology seems inevitable in terms of lowering management costs. The governing side's logic is that it is a win-win situation; directing workers toward desirable behavior and a state of happiness is a version of paternalism, but it is still questionable in that workers are subjugated without their awareness. On the other hand, those who can't adapt to this type of management face utilitarianism's so-called "Trolly Problem," in which a minority of

individuals are discarded in favor of the majority.

Community style, a place of inclusion

Australia, which was one of the first countries to adopt ABW from the Netherlands, in the 2000s, and is now a global front-runner building its own unique approach, seems to be coping well with the issue of the "degradation of emotions." Let's take a look at some examples.

Aiming to become the number-one digital bank, CBA used their recent relocation as a chance to consolidate their tech talent. Workers are provided an environment that allows them to achieve a highly technology-oriented work style, but, before that, the first and most important thing is "community." The offices are in an area that has its own narrative, and they're designed to be "good neighbors" by creating spaces to contribute to the community. In addition, the interior is designed to be a reliable place for workers that precedes technology, with plenty of spaces that support this community.

Paramount House attempts to create a visible "new church" for people who share the same postcode. Their target audience are Millennials and digital natives. Rather than using technology to solve issues in the neighborhood, they created an enriched living environment by hand-picking meaningful tenants. A lively world of conversations between neighbors and business meetings unfolds daily in the café that is open to the street.

It's impossible to list them all here, but this issue's case studies see smart technology as a means to an end, and prioritize and invest

in creating a better community of their own above all else. I would also like to highlight the awareness of "placemaking" that fosters comfortable spaces where you want to belong. Exceptional places attract people and lead to rich shared experiences. A common experience isn't necessarily a conversation shared amongst a group or a shared activity: the main point is that the place itself fosters a sense of inclusion for everyone who steps into it. That sense of inclusion and even a small amount of consideration toward other members of the community can prevent the "degradation of emotions."

Although it wasn't seen among the cases in this issue, there is also a movement toward creating spaces of inclusion through technology. For instance, "platform corporatism" is an effort to create a cooperative that is operated through technology.

I would also like to point out that behind the creation of such communities is the importance of individual desires and goals. As a global lifestyle powerhouse, Australia is home to organizations that want to support or create these communities because its workers each have a clear image of the life they want to lead. A lifestyle that integrates individual lifestyles—a "community style," if you will—has been born.

When people lose their sense of will, technology is going to take meaning away from our lives and our work. In Australia, there is a culture that prevents this from happening. Humans must not let technology get the best of us. **WS**

BACK ISSUES

バックナンバー

WORKSIGHT のバックナンバーは、書店、amazon.co.jp または
渋谷ヒカリエ 8F の Creative Lounge MOV の店頭にてお買い求めいただけます。

WORKSIGHT
創刊準備号
特集
境界を越える発想
The Hub
博多小学校
三つ葉在宅クリニック
2010 年 11 月 12 日発行
非売品

SOLD OUT

WORKSIGHT 01
特集
外とのつながりで
発想するオフィス
Zappos ／ Gore
Ziba ／日建設計
ライフネット生命
隠岐郡海士町
2011 年 10 月 7 日発行
定価 1,200 円（税抜）

SOLD OUT

WORKSIGHT 02
特集
オーガニック・
コミュニケーション
HOK ／ Innocent Drinks
Arup ／ Acne Production
DDB Stockholm
Hyper Island
サイバーエージェント
2012 年 6 月 28 日発行
定価 800 円（税抜）

SOLD OUT

WORKSIGHT 03
特集
イントラプレナーシップ
に火をつけろ！
Evernote ／ Autodesk
Skype
Wikimedia Foundation
Obscura Digital
良品計画 ／ d.school
2012 年 11 月 11 日発行
定価 800 円（税抜）

WORKSIGHT 04
特集
オープンイノベーション
で限界を超える
Rovio Entertainment
Aalto Design Factory
Sitra
Deutsche Telekom
MindLab
ReD Associates
2013 年 6 月 24 日発行
定価 800 円（税抜）

SOLD OUT

WORKSIGHT 05
特集
ソーシャル・
コネクティビティ
QVC ジャパン ／ GSK
Continuum ／ Tumblr
Acumen
Green Spaces
2013 年 12 月 16 日発行
定価 800 円（税抜）

WORKSIGHT 06
特集
レジリエント・
ワークスタイル
NHN Entertainment
Singapore Telecom
Seoul Creative Lab
id KAIST ／ Asiance
The Co
2014 年 10 月 1 日発行
定価 800 円（税抜）

WORKSIGHT 特別号
特集
これからの働く環境を
考える 7 つの視点
Design ／ Management
Innovation Technology
Facility Management
Learning Environment
Future Insights
2014 年 12 月 26 日発行
定価 700 円（税抜）

WORKSIGHT 07
特集
セルフメイド・
フューチャー
Essent ／ NDSM
Spaces ／ Royal Dutch
Shell ／ Waag Society
／ Seats2meet.com
2015 年 4 月 22 日発行
定価 800 円（税抜）

WORKSIGHT 08
特集
ウェルビーイング・
アット・ワーク
Medibank ／ NAB
SAHMRI
Macquarie Group
Envato ／ tacsi
2015 年 10 月 16 日発行
定価 800 円（税抜）

WORKSIGHT 09
特集
クリエイティブ
スクールの未来
The York University
The University of
British Columbia
The University of
Toronto ／ Microsoft
MEC ／ Telus
2016 年 4 月 19 日発行
定価 800 円（税抜）

WORKSIGHT 10
特集
エコシステムを生む
ワークプレイス
Zappos.com,
Downtown Project
SAP, HanaHaus
Square
Dolby Laboratories
Cisco
2016 年 10 月 31 日発行
定価 800 円（税抜）

WORKSIGHT 11
特集
スタートアップ都市
ベルリンの
ネクストステップ
betahaus ／ Factory
Wooga
Axel Springer Plug &
Play Accelerator
IXDS ／ Tech Open Air
2017 年 4 月 24 日発行
定価 1,000 円（税抜）

WORKSIGHT 12
特集
レガシーと
革新のロンドン
Barclays ／ Sky
The Collective
Level39
Future Cities Catapult
Here East
2017 年 12 月 18 日発行
定価 1,000 円（税抜）

WORKSIGHT 13
特集
コミュニティ・ドリブン
都市 ニューヨーク
Kickstarter ／ Boston
Consulting Group
Vice ／ A/D/O
Industry City
Pilotworks
2018 年 6 月 22 日発行
定価 1,000 円（税抜）

WORKSIGHT 14
特集
台北 集まり方の流儀
CIT
Gamania Group
松山文創園区
FutureWard
Fieldoffice Architects
Taiwan Startup Stadium
PDIS
2019 年 1 月 10 日発行
定価 1,500 円（税抜）

WORKSIGHT 特別号
特集
Studio O+A が生んだ
ワークプレイス新時代
McDonald's ／ Slack
Blend
Cambridge Associates
Microsoft ／ Abaca
Giant Pixel
Alibaba Group
2019 年 7 月 25 日発行
定価 1,800 円（税抜）

WORKSIGHT 15
特集
スマートワーク
プレイスの未来
Edge Olympic Amsterdam
22 Bishopsgate
Microsoft Netherlands
CIRCL ／ B. Amsterdam
Superblocks
2020 年 3 月 25 日発行
定価 1,500 円（税抜）